Praise for
Does Every Woman Have an Eating Disorder?

"Stacey Rosenfeld has written a smart, important, and wildly necessary book. It should be required reading for all women—and the men in their lives."

—*Abby Ellin, author of* Teenage Waistland

"Dr. Rosenfeld's book is a must-read for girls and women across race, class, and age. Blending sociology and psychology, she couples a critical analysis on everything from the cult of celebrity and the role of advertising to body image concerns across the life span with engaging and eye-opening exercises. I'll definitely be using this in my classes and as reference in my own work as a body image advocate."

—*Melanie Klein, Professor of Sociology and Women's Studies, Santa Monica College, and coeditor of* Yoga and Body Image

"In asking whether every woman has an eating disorder, Stacey Rosenfeld shows that disordered eating and body image problems are much more common than statistics about full-blown eating disorders would suggest. Rosenfeld shows how these problems stem from the incessant negative messages propagated by mainstream contemporary US culture. Insightful and incisive, *Does Every Woman Have an Eating Disorder?* also offers practical advice for developing a positive relationship with food and feeling comfortable in one's own skin. Highly recommended for anyone who has ever dieted or felt ashamed of how her body looks."

—*Abigail C. Saguy, Associate Professor of Sociology, UCLA, and author of* What's Wrong with Fat?

"An important addition to the field. Stacey Rosenfeld illuminates how our toxic cultural environment contributes to disordered eating and attitudes toward food and our bodies. And she offers some useful strategies for change."

—*Jean Kilbourne, EdD, Senior Scholar, Wellesley Centers for Women and creator of the* Killing Us Softly: Advertising's Image of Women *film series*

"Dr. Rosenfeld insightfully exposes the reader to the often neglected world of women and disordered eating. Many conflicted and hurting women who do not have a full-fledged eating disorder but still struggle with weight and body image will find enormous comfort and a door to freedom in this well-written book."

—*Jacquelyn Ekern, MS, LPC, President, Eating Disorder Hope*

"Dr. Rosenfeld does a great job of addressing the concerns most women have about weight and eating and provides useful strategies to the reader for improving her relationship with food and her body. I will be recommending the book to my clients."

—*Lauren Muhlheim, PsyD, Psychologist and Certified Eating Disorder Specialist*

"Stacey Rosenfeld and her terrific book just made my job easier. As an advocate supporting people who experience weight bias and weight stigma, I often find it difficult to slice through the rhetoric of 'common knowledge' when speaking with people who aren't aware there is another side to the story. Dr. Stacey concisely breaks down that 'knowledge' and bite by bite discredits the fallacies while building a new foundational knowledge of accurate, scientifically proven fact that people can in turn build better self-image, habits of proper self-care, and decisions that work best for their body upon."

—*Lizabeth Wesely-Casella, founder of BingeBehavior.com*

"Stacey Rosenfeld adeptly captures the current science about eating and body image and delivers it in a meaningful, relatable style. This highly valuable resource will resonate with clinicians, parents, women, and essentially everyone who eats!"

—*Hope W. Levin, MD, Psychiatrist*

"Stacey Rosenfeld has presented us with an approachable, insightful, and practical book to help women explore their relationships to food, their bodies, and themselves. I really love the hands-on activities that she offers and have used several with my clients to great effect. I appreciate the personal anecdotes as well as accounts from real women on their struggles to find a peaceful relationship with food, and I'm encouraged to find that Dr. Rosenfeld offers much hope to women of all shapes, sizes, colors, and backgrounds that recovery is possible."

—*Kate B. Daigle, MA, NCC, LPC, Licensed Professional Counselor and Eating Disorder Specialist*

"Dr. Rosenfeld shines a light on the incredibly 'normal' problem of body image dissatisfaction that women today face in epidemic proportions. Her words echo the true notion that women are capable and valuable for more than what they look like, and once they recognize the ways negative body image holds them back from their full potential, they can get somewhere much more empowering and liberating."

—*Lexie Kite, PhD, cofounder of the Beauty Redefined Foundation*

Does Every Woman Have an Eating Disorder?

///

Stacey M. Rosenfeld, PhD

SIENA MOON BOOKS

Siena Moon Books
11301 W. Olympic Blvd., #307
Los Angeles, CA 90064
www.sienamoonbooks.com

Quantity sales. Special discounts are available on quantity purchases by corporations, associations, and others. For details, contact the "Special Sales Department" at the address above.

Orders by US trade bookstores and wholesalers. Please contact BCH: (800) 431-1579 or visit www.bookch.com for details.

Printed in the United States of America

HAES is a registered copyright of the Association for Size Diversity and Health (ASDAH).

Cataloging-in-Publication Data
    Rosenfeld, Stacey M.
        Does every woman have an eating disorder? : challenging our nation's fixation with food and weight /
        Stacey M. Rosenfeld, PhD.—First edition.
        pages cm
        Includes bibliographical references and index.
        LCCN 2014931486
        ISBN 9780989851831 (print book)
        ISBN 9780989851848 (e-book)
        1. Eating disorders in women. 2. Body image in women. 3. Women—Psychology.
I. Title.
    RC552.E18R67 2014   616.85'26
    QBI14-600023

First Edition

18 17 16 15 14   10 9 8 7 6 5 4 3 2 1

To JB and EF, who arrived
at exactly the right time

⫽ Contents

⁄⁄⁄ Preface

IS THIS BOOK FOR YOU, even if you don't think you have an eating disorder? Let's see.

This book is for the woman who at some point or another has disliked her stomach or breasts or butt or thighs or hips or legs and therefore herself and therefore her life.

It's for the woman who spends any portion of her day reviewing her caloric intake, overexercising, craving, munching, starving, picking, overeating, dieting, withholding, nibbling, and comparing herself to others—then waking up the next morning to do it all over again.

It's for the woman who repeats this cycle over and over, sometimes for years, even as a small, healthy voice inside her issues a muffled scream: "Stop!"

If you recognize yourself in any of the above statements, you might have a disordered approach to eating or poor body image. You're not alone. Most women living in our culture struggle with this issue. According to one study, 80 percent of women are dissatisfied with their appearance.[1]

Over my fifteen years of clinical training and practice, across thousands of clinical hours counseling women, I have met so many souls struck by the eating disorder bug: restricting, bingeing, vomiting, abusing laxatives, overexercising, pathologically dieting, and approaching the body and psyche with self-reproach and often disgust. What may surprise you is that it's not just women diagnosed with anorexia or bulimia who obsess about shape or size. Weight-controlling behaviors are common to "normal" women, too—just to a lesser degree and sometimes under a different name. Counting calories, eliminating carbs or fat or sugar from your diet, juicing, cleansing, scheduling an extra workout to burn off that cheesecake, and thinking of your self-worth in terms of your dress size or the number on a scale can all be forms of disordered behavior. Everyday eating behaviors like these might not be classified per the *Diagnostic and Statistical Manual of Mental Disorders* as a medical or mental illness (though, based on frequency and severity, they can be classified as an other specified feeding and eating disorder or an unspecified feeding and eating disorder), but they can take away from your quality of life. Consider the following scenario:

You go to dinner at a well-rated new restaurant you've been hoping to visit for weeks. You sit down and open the menu. Everything sounds delicious. You want one of everything. But you're not focused on choosing what you crave—you're thinking about what you deserve. What have you already eaten that day? How much have you exercised? How much should you limit yourself to now? As you read through the appetizers and entrées, you link moral states to your menu choices ("I should be good"). If you make one "wrong" choice (dinner roll, pasta, dessert), you feel guilty. Self-contempt for your "sinful" behavior can be enough to rocket you into an outright binge later on ("Bring on the bag of chips!"). You have these thoughts and behaviors so often, they're second nature whether you're thin or heavy—but God help you if you make "bad" choices while you're already overweight. The frustration you feel as a result of your "mistake" can undo your resolve to even try controlling your intake.

That's still not me, you might be thinking. Maybe you're right, but I don't know one woman who doesn't think or talk more than is necessary about food, her weight, or her body. If you're a woman, you've probably already had one such conversation today, either with others or yourself.

Maybe it's time we changed that conversation.

The first step is to admit that body image and self-esteem issues affect all of us to some degree. Surprisingly, this step can be harder than you'd think. I can cite an example from my days as a postdoctorate fellow at a university in suburban New York. As part of our campus outreach, a colleague and I created a three-part workshop targeted at body image and eating disorder concerns. Our plan was to offer this workshop to the college population. Campuses can breed body dissatisfaction, and eating disorders are rampant. We knew there was a problem and we had ideas about how to fix it, including popular exercises (self-esteem pies, anyone?). We advertised the workshop, and when the big day arrived, we were prepared and ready to educate, enlighten, and empathize.

Two people came.

On another college campus, I held a similar workshop. Five people came. When I asked that group of five why they thought other students didn't attend such programming, one woman answered, "Because it's embarrassing."

I didn't give up. I presented my workshops in other venues and cities. Whenever attendance was mandatory (i.e., in a psychology class), the room would be fiery and alive with ideas as young women talked about the problems of their roommates, their friends, and their relatives. They talked about how our society encouraged disordered eating and body image obsession. They talked so much about so many issues that we ran out of time. It turned out that women *will* talk about disordered eating and body image issues—as long as they're talking about someone else's issues, not their own.

But these issues affect all of us. If you are a woman in a Western culture, and increasingly in other cultures as well, you probably experience harmful body dissatisfaction to some degree. If you act on this dissatisfaction by denying yourself pleasure, punishing yourself with workouts, or accepting chronic hunger as a normal state of being (instead of eating when you're hungry), then I posit that you *do* have an eating disorder. The reason you've been unaware of it until now is that the problem is so widespread and so culturally acceptable that these associated behaviors are perceived as normal. As a society, we promote the desire to be thin. We think, does a woman who counts calories really have a problem? Isn't a compulsive runner just being healthy? Why does a woman who significantly restricts her intake need help if she's praised and reinforced and looks like a runway model?

In our culture, anyone who questions the drive to be thin is swimming upstream. Eating disorders and body image issues don't get the same compassionate support that other compulsive behaviors do. The support networks we offer for substance abuse, for instance, don't exist in the same rally-cry way for eating problems, and perversely, often the group environments that do exist, unless professionally and sensitively run, fail because the very nature of eating disorders makes competition likely in a group. Some studies show that group interventions can lead to peer imitation (picking up new "tricks"), triggering and reinforcement of the eating disordered behaviors, and in a worst-case scenario, competition to become the thinnest member of the group.[2] In the battle of the bulge, the woman who weighs the least wins the war. This is a fight we're all in, and in some cases, it's a fight to the death. That's what we've created.

The good news is, we can uncreate it. Body dissatisfaction is a problem that has a solution. Treatment of body image issues, eating disorders, or compulsive eating does not have to stay in the dark. We can each help one another.

In psychology, we use the word "normalize." When you find out someone has had an experience similar to yours, you exclaim (often with relief), "Oh, you do that?" When we realize that others are in a similar boat, we take comfort in learning that we're not abnormal. My hope is that through open and honest discussion, we can normalize food fixation and body hatred, weakening their grip on our lives and freeing us of our obsessions. To that end, this book seeks to inform, to share, and to offer suggestions for how we can fight the forces that contribute to the disordered relationships with food, appearance, or body size or shape common to almost every woman.

Chapter 1 begins with a description of the problem and its prevalence— how women come to dislike their bodies and to fixate, instead, on the "perfect body." Chapter 2 focuses on the range of behaviors, thoughts, and feelings that define disordered eating. I pay specific attention here to disordered behaviors that may not arouse clinical attention but are still consuming, distressing, and oftentimes dangerous. Chapters 3–5 explore the cultural forces that contribute to disordered eating, including our language related to food and weight, the role of celebrity worship, and our collective incrimination of fat, which we attack unnecessarily under the guise of promoting good health. Chapter 6 traces women's disordered eating throughout their lifetime, from infancy to old age. Chapter 7 draws upon feminist ideologies, addressing why women compose the majority of eating disorder cases. Finally, chapter 8 examines how we can change the way we think about our bodies and how we treat them and, by extension, how we treat ourselves.

I would be remiss as a mental health professional to discuss such a widespread concern without offering thoughts as to how to remedy the situation, at both the individual and collective levels. Throughout this book, you will find exercises and tips to help you think differently about your relationships with food and your body, culminating in a list of 10 Practices in chapter 8. While these exercises and practices should not be used at the expense of in-person consultation with a clinician, they can guide those who need it into treatment and offer some encouragement and perceptual shifts for those ready to make a change.

Sharing our stories is the first and perhaps most important tool we have. Even though I'm a therapist, I'm not immune to the experiences I describe in this book. "Research is me-search," academics like to say, and I plead guilty. At various points in my life, I have undereaten, overeaten, overexercised, and judged and criticized my shape and size. Because I can relate to the struggle, I refer to several of my personal experiences throughout this book, particularly where I feel they might be helpful or illustrative to others.

I also include case studies and stories from other women, garnered from my blog *Does Every Woman Have an Eating Disorder* (www .everywomanhasaneatingdisorder.blogspot.com). Shortly after I began work on this manuscript, I decided to publish segments of it online in an effort to keep myself motivated and to solicit feedback from curious readers. With no previous blogging experience, I didn't know what to expect. The results surprised and sometimes shocked me. As I describe in chapter 3, many readers found my blog while searching for celebrity diets and dress sizes or—appallingly—tips for acquiring and maintaining an eating disorder.

Fortunately, many more women found it while searching for a place to talk about eating and body image issues in a constructive and healthy space. Over time, I attracted a cadre of devoted readers who blessed me often with comments that served as portals into their personal lives. A number of these regular readers helped give birth to an active "Does Every Woman Have an Eating Disorder?" community.

Throughout this book, I allude often to comments that women so graciously shared with this community. Their participation helped me to crystallize my ideas and gave me new ones to explore. When I mentioned that I was writing a book, several readers, without prompting, e-mailed me their personal stories. With their permission, I share some of their thoughts and experiences with you. I am forever grateful to each woman who allowed me access to her world. I hope you will, as I did, connect to these stories and feel supported and inspired. By sharing our common experiences, I believe we can all come to a place where we can challenge the status quo, accept our bodies as they are, and support one another in achieving goals that aren't related to food and weight.

CHAPTER 1

⁄⁄⁄ In Search of the Perfect Body

To lose confidence in one's body
is to lose confidence in oneself.
—SIMONE DE BEAUVOIR

AS A THERAPIST, during my customary evaluation with new patients, I always ask about eating disorders. Typically, the response is yes or no— either a patient has struggled with an eating disorder or she hasn't. A couple of patients have surprised me with their answers, saying, in effect, "Aside from the ordinary?" In just one quip, these patients echoed what I'd been researching and thinking about for years. To be "disordered" about eating and our bodies is, at this time and in this place, rather ordinary.

Almost every woman has an eating disorder of sorts—not necessarily anorexia, bulimia, or binge eating per se, but a fixation on food, weight, and shape that is unhealthy, unwanted, and undying. Can you imagine a day, or even a meal, without thinking at least one of the following?

- Can I eat this?

- I shouldn't.

- What have I eaten already?

- Have I exercised today?

- I wonder how many calories this has.

- What's she eating?

- I've had too much.

- Does this make me look fat?

- I hate my [insert body part].

You're not alone. Twenty million women and ten million men struggle with an eating disorder at some point during their lives.[1] According to one widely circulated statistic, an estimated 54 percent of us would rather be hit by a truck than be fat.[2] More than half of us would rather be maimed by a heavy automobile than risk going up a few jeans sizes, but still, we don't think we have a problem. We're so accustomed to thinking *thinner is better* that our disordered thoughts and behaviors seem to be perfectly normal.

Though we accept this thinner-is-better concept as a given, in reality, our cultural preference for female thinness is a relatively new phenomenon. If you look at the sizes of models, movie stars, Miss America contestants, and even *Playboy* centerfolds over the last fifty years, you'll see sharp decreases in weight during the second half of the twentieth century. Even our mannequins have shrunk. In 1950, the hip measurement for store mannequins was 34 inches, reflecting the size of the average woman at the time. Forty years later, when heroin chic descended on the fashion catwalk, mannequins' hips shrunk to 31 inches—even though the average hip measurement for real women climbed to 37 inches.[3] As we have grown, our goal size has gotten smaller. Today, the average American woman is 5 feet 4 inches tall and weighs 166 pounds, whereas the average Miss America winner is three inches taller and weighs 121 pounds.[4] Most mainstream clothing stores house up to size 12 clothing, some only up to 10. Sizes larger than this are relegated to plus-size stores. The average American woman wears a size 14, meaning the average American woman is considered too big to shop in the average American store.

Given these facts, it's no surprise that the frequency of eating disorders has increased.[5] Since 1930, every decade has seen a rise in the incidence of anorexia in young women ages 15 to 19, and between 1988 and 1993, the incidence of bulimia in women ages 10 to 39 tripled.[6] As the size we aspire to ratchets downward, we're racing to be thinner. "Fat," to many women, has become the worst thing we can be. In her movie *Jesus Is Magic*, comedienne Sarah Silverman jokes, "I don't care if you think I'm racist as long as you don't think I'm fat."[7] It's only funny because it's true. Women would rather hear a host of negative, pejorative labels about themselves than the word "fat": "conniving," "bitchy," "anxious," "sad," "cunning," and "mean" are all unfortunate identifiers, but none as personally offensive as the f-word.

Proof of this fear of fat became even more evident to me when I asked my blog readers to free-associate to the word "fat." Their responses: fat is "gross," "sloppy," "lazy," "disgusting," "ugly," "misery," and "worthless."

"Thin," however, was a different story. "Thin" was associated with the words "grace," "elegant," "feminine," "beauty," "admirable," "happiness," "light," "self-controlled," and "more worthy."

More worthy of what? I wondered. Happiness? When I asked another group of women, "Would you rather be happy or thin?" one responded, "What's the difference?"

American women have internalized a cultural link between thinness and everything else we value. Do you want a successful career? A devoted spouse? An engaging group of friends? Be thin and everything else will fall into place. The closer women are to skinny, the more graceful, beautiful, feminine, motivated, happy, and worthy we are—or so we believe.

In *Fat Is a Feminist Issue: The Anti-Diet Guide for Women*, Susie Orbach effectively sums up the fantasies of every woman who wants to be thin: "We shall be light enough to sit on someone's knee and lithe enough to dance. If we stand out in a crowd it will be because we are lovely, not 'repulsive.' We shall sit down in any position comfortably, not worrying where the flab shows. We shall sweat less and smell nicer."[8]

Most women I work with in therapy have the idea that if they could just be thinner, life would be perfect. But thin women are still concerned with how they look and smell, the images they project, and approval from friends, family, and strangers. They still at times feel disempowered, dissatisfied, and ashamed of their bodies. And certainly, as they are culturally instructed to do, they still make excuses for their eating. The danger with wanting to be thinner is that there's always room for less of you. As one of my blog readers pointed out, "I don't think we all have the same idea of what a perfect body is, but we all think that we need to lose weight, regardless of what we look like now."

The Perfect Body

If our desire for thinness and an admirable physique were simply about achieving good health, our national obsession might not be so dangerous to women's wellness and self-esteem. But it seems we're driven less by health concerns than by the desire to reach an aesthetic ideal, a desire that's funded by multibillion-dollar diet, fitness, and cosmetic surgery industries.

How often do you find yourself flipping through a fashion magazine and pointing out a "perfect body" to a friend? The desire has taken root. A quick Internet search reveals hundreds of sites and images that refer to the "perfect body" (usually with near-naked women lounging around) along with a number of tips designed to help us achieve this saintly state. But what is the perfect body, exactly? When perfection is so subjective, do we actually agree on a single definition?

One of my blog readers commented astutely, "Do all women have the same idea of what is a perfect body? Or just the same idea that they shouldn't like the body that they already have?" Another commented that all women are united in not feeling "our own personal best."

While individuals might disagree on what perfect means, an informal survey of television shows and magazine advertisements confirms a trend. The perfect female body, as traditionally defined by Madison Avenue, is thin with large breasts, a flat stomach, slim hips, and a tight butt. It's tanned and toned but not so tanned as to wrinkle and not so toned as to be muscular.

IS THINNER BETTER?

How many thin people do you know who are truly happier, more successful, more fulfilled, and more comfortable in their skin than their heavier colleagues or friends? I know plenty of happy, coupled, confident, funny women who are heavier than today's ideal. I also know plenty of single, stuck, dissatisfied women who happen to be thin.

There should be curves but not too many or too big. The perfect body is at least 5 feet 6 inches tall because taller bodies appear thinner. The face should be perfect, with large, wide-set eyes; a button nose; high cheekbones; full lips; smooth skin; and long, straight or sometimes wavy hair—blonde, of course (though the rise of certain reality stars, and Angelina Jolie, are starting to make darker hair more acceptable).[9] This is the perfect body we're exposed to regularly, perfected by Photoshop, replicated by celebrities, and condoned and appreciated by us. If we dislike any part of our own bodies by comparison, we fantasize about removing it—often in violent ways.

On my blog, I demonstrated this fantasy by sharing a common therapeutic exercise that has made the rounds in treatment and on the eating disorder and body image blogs, an apology letter to your body. I wrote a sample letter of apology to get readers started, including specific mention of a loathed body part: "I'm sorry for even briefly, and wildly, entertaining the notion that I'd like to be rid of you…and, even more so, for imagining hacking you off with a circular saw." In response, comments poured in from readers. One asked if I'd been reading her mind but indicated that the weapon of choice in her violent fantasy is a machete. Another was surprised that this was such a common fantasy and shared that in her version, she first hacks off her body part with a knife and then fries it up in a pan.

Lacking the ability to Photoshop ourselves into the perfect body, we're left with fantasies about getting the job done with butcher knives and power tools.

EXERCISE: Make Peace with Your Body Part

Think of the body part that arouses the most contempt in you, the part that, when you catch your reflection in the mirror, elicits your greatest deal of scorn. Is it your stomach? Your hips? Your arms? Your thighs? Close your eyes for several moments and think of this body part in the kindest, most loving way you can imagine. Picture this body part in your favorite color, radiating light. See if you can direct warmth and energy to it. Think of all the suffering that you've caused (and endured) as a result of disliking this part. Imagine what it feels like to be this innocent part of your body, so disliked by you. Recognize that this body part and your body as a whole are simply trying to exist in peace.

The Body-Self Link

Body criticism like this, and in its extreme form, body hatred, raise the inevitable question—can you love yourself and hate your body? Or, assuming love is an ambitious goal, is it possible to achieve self-acceptance if you haven't accepted the way you look?

Outside of your weight or shape, I'm sure there are things about your appearance that you don't find ideal but that you're willing to live with. Maybe your hair is frizzy or your complexion is spotty. Maybe your feet are funny-looking. As a personal example, I point to my fingernails. No matter what I do, they don't grow; as soon as they're about an eighth of an inch beyond my fingertips, they snag, peel, or break. Sure, I can do some things to change the situation (use nail hardeners, for example), but the bottom line is, I'm never going to have long nails. And I'm okay with that.

Why can't we be this relaxed about our body shape or weight? Why can't we casually lament that we're not supermodels, wonder what it might be like to be thinner, but stop there and accept our bodies as they are?

When I asked this question on my blog, one reader commented that she used to think of these two arenas as separate, that she loved herself but disliked her body. Now, however, she realizes that "my 'self' and my 'body' are interconnected."

Her response recalls the earlier word-association assignment. "Fat" carries with it a list of negative synonyms. If we think we are fat, don't we also think we are all those other words? How often do you make the distinction in your mind between your body and yourself? By disliking our bodies, we end up disliking ourselves. The reverse is also true. One of my blog readers wrote that when she was hating and mistreating her body, she was really just hating herself. She realized that her body "was just a casualty of war."

Body dissatisfaction so easily turns emotional and destructive. Nothing packs the same emotional punch as not weighing what we think we should. Nothing has such a grip, such a soul clamp, on who we are as the gap between how our bodies are and how we want them to be.

. . . .

ASSIGNMENT: Honor Your Strengths

Every time I meet with a new patient, I ask her, "What do you like about yourself? What would you say are your personal strengths?"

How would you answer this question? Make a list of what you honor and enjoy about yourself. This is not a time to be modest! If your list is short, or if you aren't confident in your answers, focus on how you can expand upon your strengths. Ask your friends and family what they like most about you. Think about the positive feedback you've been given through the years. The more identified you are with your personal strengths, the less pressure you may feel for your body to be perfect.

. . . .

Striving for Less

If you believe that thinner is better and you want to be better (and happier and more successful), how far are you willing to go to lose weight? Many women dream about bartering other parts of their lives in exchange for the "magic pill" of thinness. A study conducted for *Fitness* magazine showed that among 1,007 men and women questioned, more than 50 percent would rather lose their jobs than gain weight. Specifically, 58 percent of the women would rather be let go than gain 75 pounds.[10] Personally, I find some small degree of comfort in that number. Seventy-five pounds is a major weight gain, not just 5 or 10 pounds. Maybe the study participants—men, too—were looking for a reason to change careers.

But before I get too optimistic, let me share some other statistics from the study. More than 25 percent of the women polled would rather have their wisdom teeth extracted than go shopping for bathing suits. Twenty-five percent of women and 20 percent of men indicated they'd sacrifice 20 IQ points for the perfect body. Some people would drop from an assumed average IQ of 100 to an IQ of 80, just above borderline intellectual functioning, rather than settle for a less-than-perfect figure.[11]

If this study is to be believed, the average woman is willing to experience painful surgery, a reduction in intellect, and unemployment rather than be heavy. Given the bias our culture has for beauty (see "The Perfect Body," above), these choices aren't too surprising. Being heavy carries with it negative social judgments toward women, and we internalize that negativity, punishing ourselves if we don't fit the ideal.

Being fat can cause economic and career penalties, as well. Most of us have heard the stories about how pretty girls finish first. Studies show that in the workplace, attractive women may be hired before and many earn more money than their less-attractive counterparts.[12] According to Abby Ellin's 2007 *New York Times* article "When the Food Critics Are Deskside," one owner of a headhunting firm in New York said, "When I'm interviewing someone and I see their bones protruding, I know it's a good hire."[13] In a work climate where a small frame is thought by some to be a better predictor of success than brainpower, it's no wonder women would be willing to literally lose their minds in order to be thin.

Landing the job is no guarantee that you're done running the weight gauntlet at work. In the same article, Ellin went on to say, "No matter how private you think it is, what you eat—and how much—sends telltale signals. People make assumptions about your character, whether you're driven (grilled salmon) or lazy (pepperoni pizza)."[14] I saw this firsthand at my first real job. One day at the lunch table, the inevitable diet talk began: a discussion about the calorie contents of our various frozen entrées. One colleague's frozen meal measured in at almost 400 calories, causing her distress. "That's not that much," I campaigned.

My coworker countered, "It's not that much for you—you work out." I was the only one in the room larger than a size 2.

Despite all our fantasies of *more*—more time, more love, more connectedness, more patience, more kindness, more money (and probably, more food)—really, when it comes to ourselves, what we're looking for is *less*. Even the women who are held up as our body ideals are suffering from this drive. During the course of writing this book, I watched as the international size 0 debate emerged. Gone are the days where women with flesh walked the runway and fit into sample sizes. Now even a size 6 is considered plus-size in the fashion industry, and clothing stores offer size 00, raising the proverbial bar for skinniness.[15] As our literal and figurative perfect body models continue to shrink, everyday women who aspire to be like them flirt dangerously close to nothingness. Women used to strive simply to be smaller; now our goal is literally to be less than zero.

OSFED: The Catchall Eating Disorder

Living as we do in a culture that practically dictates the need to become smaller, I'd be surprised if you were not affected by the hordes of thinness directives we receive on a daily basis. If you worry about your weight, welcome to the club. Here's something you might not realize, however: the collective drive to get or stay thin can contribute to real, diagnosable eating disorders. Other Specified Feeding and Eating Disorder (OSFED) is a psychiatric catchall designed to classify people with disordered behavior who don't meet the full criteria for anorexia, bulimia, or binge-eating disorder or who present with variations in pathology. You might be diagnosed with OSFED if you restrict your food but are still at a normal weight; if you periodically misuse laxatives, diuretics, or other medications in an effort to control your weight; or if you binge (or binge and purge), but not often enough to be diagnosed with bulimia or binge-eating disorder. If any of your behaviors around food or weight significantly and negatively impact your life, this also qualifies as disordered.

Now let's remove disordered behaviors from the equation. According to the American Psychiatric Association, some of the mental/psychological symptoms of anorexia nervosa and/or bulimia nervosa include

- Extreme fear of weight gain (even in the face of significantly low weight, as in the case with anorexia)
- Distorted views of one's weight or shape
- Self-concept excessively influenced by weight or shape[16]

How many of these have you experienced this week?

In her memoir, *Life Inside the "Thin" Cage: A Personal Look into the Hidden World of the Chronic Dieter*, Constance Rhodes talks about women with some sort of unspecified eating disorder, including herself, who "never reach the behavioral extremes but live in a never-ending nightmare of the in between, obsessed with weight and preoccupied with looking a certain way."[17]

An example of OSFED comes from one of my blog readers, Chelsea. Chelsea, a lifelong athlete, began dieting when she was a petite high school freshman, after her brother told her, "You can stand to lose 5 pounds." Chelsea tried different eating patterns to keep her calories in check, including a carb-only phase where all she would eat was bread. She lost the 5 pounds and more but still judged herself as fat. Exercise, including daily StairMaster workouts, became central to her life. Chelsea relished comments on her weight loss and felt particularly good when a friend's mother told her that her hipbones were jutting out.

Now, years later and back near her starting weight, Chelsea thinks she overeats; friends think she doesn't eat enough. On an average day, on a "body love" scale of 1 to 100 (100 being "I love my body"), she says she ranks a 4. She still works out at least ninety minutes per day ("I freak out if I miss a day") and weighs herself daily, fifteen times on average. She says, "I spend most of the day worrying or thinking about my body and how I look or feel. I probably spend 90 percent of my day thinking about it."

Chelsea has never been diagnosed with anorexia, bulimia, or binge-eating disorder, as she has never met sufficient criteria. She says, "Sometimes I do think I have [a disorder], if I start to think about all the crazy stuff I do to try and lose weight. Most of the time I don't because I see myself. I'm not skinny, and I do eat. It's not like I starve myself....I guess I don't really have a real eating disorder." Still, Chelsea admits, "The thought of eating scares me sometimes. All I know is that I need to lose 10 lbs and I want my bones to stick out."

Although Chelsea's body dissatisfaction and relationship to food may not exactly be typical, her case study is a good example of variations of eating disorder that can often go unnoticed. Some of her thoughts may echo feelings you've had about your own body. In my experience, almost every woman demonstrates some disordered eating or body image dissatisfaction at some point in her life—not just my patients but also friends and family, colleagues, strangers, whomever. If you are aware of your body and its flaws, if you have tried a number of diets, pills, or exercises in an effort to get your body to conform to a certain ideal, if your mood can plummet after viewing an unflattering photo of yourself or trying on a pair of jeans that feels too tight, and particularly if you are so consumed by what you are or are not eating and how much you weigh that other aspects of your life—career, family, social life, self-esteem, inner peace—become compromised, you are in good company. For many women, dieting, constricting, and restricting is a full-time job.

A friend in college once jokingly remarked to me, "If I could take all the time I've spent so far trying to lose weight and manage my body hair..." The sentence was incomplete, but her meaning was clear. We have so many better things to think about.

EXERCISE: What Might You Accomplish?

How much mental energy do you expend each day thinking about your weight and size? How much time goes into self-evaluation, self-incrimination, and self-flagellation? If you stopped thinking about your body for a full day, what might you accomplish?

One of my blog readers speculated, "I would have been able to, geez, I don't know what...explore the whole universe."

Conclusion

At an addictions conference I attended in 2006, Dr. Wendy Miller began her talk by referring to eating "disorders" as eating "problems" and asking whether we can really call something that affects 90 percent of women a disorder.[18] I agree. If your relationship with food is both "normal" and "disordered," can we really call it a pathology? Yes, but not yours. It's my belief that the pathology lies within our culture. Advertising, the media, and everyday conversations promote the persistent message that "fat is bad and thin is good." You are born into and you mature within a cultural framework that encourages you to dislike your body and therefore yourself at every stage of your life.

In the next few chapters, I look closely at this cultural framework—how it's built, how residing within it leads to a disordered mind-set and behavioral repertoire, and what steps you can take to counteract its negative impact on your life.

CHAPTER 2

⁂ Signs and Symptoms of Everyday Disordered Eating

Weight and body oppression is oppressive to everyone....
Nobody wins in this kind of struggle.
— GOLDA PORETSKY

DAVID LANDES, author and professor of economics and history, writes, "This world is divided roughly into three kinds of nations: those that spend lots of money to keep their weight down; those whose people eat to live; and those whose people don't know where their next meal is coming from."[1] Like me, you probably live in the first type of nation, where the size of your hips is more of a pressing daily concern than the source of your next meal. I am not trying to make you feel guilty for having enough; on the contrary, I fully recognize that for women with eating problems (and again, I maintain that this is most women), the constant availability of food in unimaginable quantities can be torturous. Your culture surrounds you with an abundance of food and food-oriented occasions. This same culture then tells you there's virtue in denying this abundance.

In *Life Without Ed*, Jenni Schaefer summarizes our annual festivities around food:

> Americans like to eat. And we use every holiday as an
> excuse to do just that. On the Fourth of July, we have
> barbecues. For birthdays, we light a cake on fire....We let
> our kids wander around to random houses all over town
> in search of candy on Halloween. And, of course, there
> is Thanksgiving Day—a day in which everyone acts as if
> they have an eating disorder whether they do or not. We
> like food, and we love to celebrate it.[2]

Feast is available in the United States, but famine is in. Our general surplus and celebration of food is directly opposed to the body ideal, with supersized meals challenging the size 0 less-is-more campaign.

How do today's women manage this dichotomy? The short answer is "Not very well." In my experience, most women develop highly strategized relationships with food and their bodies, relationships in which food is viewed as the enemy. To toe the line, the average woman spends a disproportionate amount of time thinking about food, having feelings about food, and developing eating-related behaviors to keep her desire for food under control. This chapter will talk about some of the daily disordered behaviors we've developed to cope with our culture's contradictory messages about food and weight. Each of these behaviors lies on a continuum, with "everyday behavior" at one end and textbook "disordered behavior" at the other. As you'll see, the difference between "normal" and "disordered" approaches to eating and food issues is often just a matter of degree.

What is truly normal and natural in a biological sense (but rare today) is physiological eating—ingesting food solely in response to hunger, as a conscious decision to keep yourself alive. When you eat out of physiological hunger, you feel your hunger arise gradually and as a function of the last time you ate. When you decide to eat, you're open to a variety of foods though you might have certain preferences. As your hunger subsides, you stop eating. You then abstain from eating until your hunger arises again.

When is the last time you remember relating to food like this? For many of us, physiological eating is something we did only in childhood, maybe even infancy. Instead, we tend to eat in response to artificial cultural cues, and we might override physiological hunger due to concerns about our weight. Left unchecked, unnatural eating habits can, in some women, lead to a continuum of behaviors ranging from today's normal abnormalities to, with genetic and temperamental proclivities in place, full-on eating disorders. I discuss the behaviors on this continuum below.

Dieting, Restrictive Eating, and Extreme Measures

Most of us have tried diets at some point in our lifetime, either for health reasons or, more commonly, to lose or manage weight. According to one study from *Nutrition Journal*, for example, approximately 83 percent of college women diet for weight loss, while research out of the United Kingdom suggests that women spend, on average, seventeen years of their lives on diets.[3] The idea behind most diets is simple: you control the quantity of food you take in over the course of each day, with the ultimate goal of losing or maintaining your weight. Diet fads come and go (more on this in chapters 4 and 5), but the basic fundamentals remain the same: you restrict yourself for a period of time by limiting what you eat. The success of our multi billion-dollar diet industry is predicated on exactly this desire to manipulate what we eat so we can control what we weigh.

Dieting is so common now that it's almost strange to meet someone who isn't on a diet. But what many people might not realize is that dieting is a close cousin (and can sometimes lead) to "restricting"—a disordered behavior typified by excessive measures to shrink one's size by limiting food. In the book *Overcoming Binge Eating*, Dr. Christopher Fairburn looks at three forms of dieting that cross over into restricting: trying not to eat for long periods of time, trying to restrict the overall amount eaten, and trying to avoid certain types of food.[4] I refer to these modes in simpler terms. Restrictive eating behavior is typified by a woman establishing "food rules" that can occur across three dimensions: when, what, and how much.

Here are some examples:

- When: You try to avoid eating before noon or after 7:00 p.m., even if your body is hungry and calling out for food.
- What: You limit your access to certain types of food like high-fat food, carbohydrates, or sweets, despite particular cravings.

- How much: You eat only half a sandwich for lunch, regardless of your hunger or satiety cues.

For the restrictive eater, such food rules trump desire, circumstance, and physiology. A restrictor obeys her rules, always. If she breaks a rule, there's a price to pay.

Many women I see in my practice will have tried various diets or will report that they have dieted on and off for years, but the restrictive eaters I see are usually much more controlled. Their rules about food are more rigid and have more of an impact on their functioning. As an example, I'm reminded of traveling with an acquaintance, Mei. By the time Mei and I arrived at our hotel's breakfast buffet, there wasn't much left besides bagels and toast. Mei, who had long shunned carbohydrates, complained that there was nothing to eat for breakfast and that she was going to go hungry until lunch. Though she typically described her food choices as healthy, on this occasion she preferred to skip breakfast (arguably an unhealthy decision) rather than eat an item on her restricted list.

Like Mei, restrictive eaters as a whole demonstrate a lack of flexibility in their food choices. Eating habits are repetitive and ritualistic. If an item is not on a restrictive eater's food list, she won't eat it and would rather go hungry. Compared to average dieters, restrictive eaters are also harder on themselves when they fail to adhere to their own rules. An ordinary dieter who cheats and eats a dessert may resume as usual the next day or may quit the diet, not really rattled by the experience. A restrictive eater who cheats may become significantly anxious, sad, or angry that she has failed. The relationship between her eating behavior and her identity and self-esteem is strong. She may feel that because she's failed to abide by her rules, she herself is a failure.

Restrictive eaters also sometimes mask their dietary rules from others— or even themselves—by saying, "I'm eating three meals a day—I'm not dieting," "I'm just being healthy," or "I'm too busy to eat." But three meals a day of low-calorie, low-carb, nonfat food items is a form of restriction, as is skipping meals—for any reason. Many women fall into this trap. If you've ever held rigid diet rules, been on a grapefruit or lemon juice diet, or felt proud to forget to eat, ask yourself, is this normal, or is it a slippery slope to disordered behavior? Dieting won't always segue into an eating disorder, but it will for some.

EXERCISE: Food Flexibility

Have there been times that you've avoided social functions or gone out to eat with family or friends but haven't participated in the group meal (whether it be splitting a pizza, sharing Chinese, or sampling everything at a dinner party) for fear of gaining weight? Can you think of any cons of not participating fully around food? Can you think of any upcoming event where you might try out being more flexible with what you eat? The goal is to be more flexible with food without somehow compensating for it before or after the event.

One of the most common disordered behaviors that can result from dieting and restriction is a diet-binge cycle that may become more and more disordered over time (see page 19 for more on this).

Another danger is that dieting can be a "gateway drug" to more extreme forms of weight and body-shape control. Over the years, diet pills and appetite suppressants in their various forms have become increasingly popular among women. In one telephone survey of more than fourteen thousand women, 7.9 percent of normal-weight respondents reported endangering their health by taking diet drugs with serious side effects.[5] In the 1990s, fen-phen, the potent combination of two weight-loss drugs, fenfluramine and phentermine, was a brief sensation, until the *New England Journal of Medicine* discovered a link between its use and mitral valve dysfunction. After numerous reports of valvular heart disease and pulmonary hypertension in women who were taking fen-phen, in 1997, the FDA recommended the removal of the drug (based on specific concerns with the fenfluramine component), along with a similar drug, dexfenfluramine (Redux), from the US market.[6] Ephedra (also known as *ma huang*) took its place until the FDA banned this drug in 2004 due to its adverse potential side effects, including heart attack, stroke, and death.[7] In 2007, Alli, an over-the-counter version of the weight-loss drug Xenical, came on the scene. Alli, which cleverly sounds like either a comrade in war or your best girlfriend, originally hit store shelves to an uproar. The fifty something–dollar starter pack sold out from pharmacies in hours. The *Los Angeles Times* interviewed Santa Monica pharmacist Roe Love, who equated the Alli sellout with the post-9/11 anthrax-induced dash to buy Cipro. The bulk of Alli purchasers at her store were women, she said, adding, "And they're not fat."[8]

Alli, which results in weight loss due to blocked fat absorption, was safe enough to get FDA approval but comes with untoward side effects. The website of the manufacturer (GlaxoSmithKline) summarizes the product's "diet-related side effects": "Such effects may include oily spotting, loose stools, and more frequent stools that may be hard to control."[9] If these side effects don't dissuade you, consider this additional warning: the product won't work without the adoption of a low-fat, low-calorie diet and a commitment to an exercise plan. Even the makers of one of today's most popular diet drugs encourage you to diet and hit the gym.

Like ephedra, most drugs marketed to women for weight loss are amphetamines or other stimulants—all of them risky and most of them addictive. In my work, I have seen women become dependent upon the psychostimulants Adderall and Ritalin after using them to lose weight. Cocaine too is popular though also highly addictive and obviously illegal. What starts out as a disordered attempt at weight management can soon become drug dependence.

The HCG diet is another new fad that combines severe calorie restriction (limiting dieters to 500 calories a day) with daily injections/sublingual administration of the hormone HCG, found in the urine of pregnant women. Promoters of this diet claim that HCG suppresses the appetite, burns body fat, and results in dramatic weight loss. However, experts state that it's the starvation diet itself that is responsible for rapid weight loss, not the HCG, and that once normal eating is resumed, the weight will return. The FDA agrees, warning that the HCG diet is dangerous and ineffective.[10]

Finally, another extreme measure women are increasingly using to control their shape is liposuction. Have you ever considered going under the wand? Liposuction has many serious risks, including (but not limited to) blood clots in the legs or lungs, infection, permanent nerve damage, and possibly fatal cardiac events.[11] But what may really make you reconsider is the side effect that might sting most: after this dangerous procedure, if you gain weight, the fat will not return to its starting place (your hips, your stomach, your thighs), but it will go somewhere—possibly somewhere even less acceptable to you than the biologically and evolutionarily intelligent places it started out.

I'll choose an hourglass shape over a distorted one any day. As a woman, your fat belongs where it is, not as an accessory to your ulna.

Emotional/Compulsive Eating, Binge Eating, and the Diet-Binge Cycle

As I mentioned earlier, one of the dangers of dieting and restricting is that this behavior can lead to a rebound of eating forbidden foods you deny yourself when you're "following the rules." Sometimes this eating is simple physical hunger in response to a period of deprivation, but often it's emotional eating (also called "compulsive eating"). Emotional eating is, essentially, eating that happens when you're not physically hungry.

Most people will eat emotionally at times. There are times that we eat with others (social eating) when we aren't physically hungry, or times when we want something comforting (e.g., macaroni and cheese) at the end of a stressful day. There are circumstances in which we eat (e.g., popcorn at a movie or ice cream on a hot summer day) even if we're not hungry because we have a particular association with food and a situation that is enjoyable to us. No one would define this as disordered. But for those who struggle with emotional/compulsive eating, such eating is more the norm than not. Emotional eaters are often involved in an epic struggle in which they use food to soothe and cope but feel guilty and miserable about the weight-gain consequences of their emotional eating.

You may be an emotional eater if you frequently eat more than you need to satisfy your hunger or if you choose certain foods based on their emotional associations—for example, cake for comfort. Emotional hunger may come on quickly and seemingly out of the blue, unrelated to the last time you ate. It typically targets a particular food or type of food in the form of immediate cravings—for example, you might feel you need to have ice cream or corn chips or jelly beans *right now!*

What makes emotional hunger tricky is that it's not physiological and therefore might not respond to physiological cues of fullness or satiety. Typically, emotional hunger will not subside once you start eating. In fact,

THE STOMACH BUG

While writing this book, I got the stomach bug. My appetite suffered and I lost weight. I asked my blog readers, "Would you secretly welcome the stomach bug in order to lose weight?" Out of 369 online votes, 138 answered, "No way!" 133 answered, "I wouldn't want it, but I'd be ok if I got it." Ninety-eight responded, "Sure!" Nearly two-thirds of respondents would be okay with suffering a virus if it meant they might drop a few pounds.

very often this hunger can seem like a void that can't be filled. For this reason, an emotional eater may, before long, find herself physically stuffed to the point of discomfort, a state that is often accompanied by feelings of guilt. This guilt, if not properly addressed, can unfortunately lead to more emotional eating, a cycle that can, in some cases, turn into binge eating.

As an example, Valerie, a 44-year-old writer and mother of two, acknowledges her struggle with emotional eating. Most of the time, Valerie eats a balanced diet, but occasionally after a particularly stressful or demanding day, while relaxing on the couch, Valerie will feel a jar of peanut butter practically calling to her from the cupboard. She might resist the urge at first, but then she'll tell herself that a little bit of peanut butter won't hurt, that she deserves a treat. One spoonful leads to many, and Valerie begins to feel uncomfortable but continues to eat. The peanut butter is sweet and salty and fun to swirl on a spoon. Like many working mothers, Valerie is either taking care of tasks or people all day long. The peanut butter ritual, though sometimes painful and always guilt-inducing, is a time that she's dedicated for herself.

EXERCISE: Emotional Eating Triggers

Emotional eating is as it sounds, eating behavior that occurs as a result of an emotional state. While these states can vary, typical triggers for emotional eating include sadness, anxiety, boredom, loneliness, and anger. Do you ever find yourself worried about something and reaching for a snack even if you aren't hungry? When you're angry, do you notice that you scrounge around for something solid that you can bite down hard into? How about when you're home alone and bored? Is this when you turn to food?

The next time you experience a difficult emotion, play around with riding it out without turning to food. Often, emotions come and go like waves, and if you wait it out a bit, you might find the urge to eat diminishes. See if you can wait a minute or maybe longer. You may end up using food to cope or you may not. Distracting yourself with a book or television show may be helpful. The more practice you get at tolerating feelings without using food, the easier it becomes—it's like strengthening an emotional muscle. And while there may be some weight-loss benefits to reducing emotional eating, the real victory lies within learning that you're strong enough to experience feelings without eating and with returning food to its rightful place, something that nourishes and provides some pleasure, but isn't a coping mechanism.

Like Valerie's emotional eating, binge eating involves consuming more food than you need to feel full and satisfied. With binge eating, however, the amount of food is larger than most people would consume on any occasion—typically enough to cause significant abdominal discomfort—and the food is typically eaten with urgency, usually in a frenetic state. Binges often start out as normal meals or snacks, but once a binge eater has eaten more than she intended, black-and-white thinking kicks in. *I've had too much*, she may think, *so I may as well have more*.

We're all guilty of this type of irrational thinking on occasion (spending money while shopping, for example), but with food, the cycle is intensified because binge eaters may derive comfort from food. They may feel that their anxious or guilty feelings from overeating can be alleviated (albeit temporarily) by continuing to eat more.

I think of Tianna as one example. Tianna is a 20-year-old college junior. Always someone who shunned breakfast because she wasn't really hungry, she decided to see if she could stretch her fast out further. *Maybe I could even skip lunch*, she wondered. She was busy anyway, running from class to class. But she also liked the idea of pushing off food—it felt like an accomplishment to her. When she skipped meals, she felt light and airy and noticed her stomach became flatter throughout the day. Some days she'd have just a small lunch, and other days she'd make it all the way through to the afternoon. *Everyone diets*, she rationalized.

By the time Tianna returned to her off-campus apartment each night, she was famished. She'd eat a normal dinner but then would find herself munching on snacks nonstop, all the way to bedtime. Each night, she'd vow to stop eating after her meal, but later she'd find herself standing in the kitchen, plundering the beckoning cupboards as if she were making up for lost time. What started as a test of will became a self-perpetuating cycle that no amount of willpower seemed to shake.

This diet-binge cycle is common among those diagnosed with eating disorders. A young woman may begin dieting and losing weight in her midteen years. In some cases, this weight loss is extreme and is tied to the development of anorexia nervosa. After some time, the woman's control over her eating starts to break down and she begins to overeat or binge in response to her deprivation. Control progressively deteriorates and her weight gradually returns to near its original level. Frustrated by this weight gain and afraid of more, she may purge or more likely, return to dieting, possibly tightening the reins to continue to chase the thin ideal. Variations of the diet-binge cycle exist, but here's the one I use:

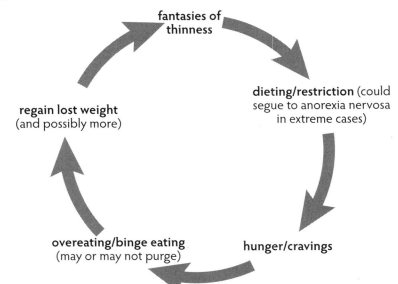

Sound familiar? When I show this graphic to women, most respond with recognition. Some have even told me, "That's the story of my life."

Why does dieting or restriction so often lead to overeating? Toward the end of World War II, a biologist/physiologist by the name of Dr. Ancel Keys answered this question in what was known as "the Minnesota starvation study." Dr. Keys's goal was to determine some of the physiological and psychological effects of restricted food intake. If he could understand the mechanisms of starvation, the world might be equipped to more adequately handle potential postwar European famine. For study participants, Keys's team signed up thirty-six physically and psychologically healthy men, conscientious objectors to the war, who volunteered to participate in a diet regimen that cut their normal caloric intake roughly in half for a period of six months. What followed was an unprecedented look into the science and psychology of malnutrition.

As captured by Todd Tucker in the book *The Great Starvation Experiment: Ancel Keys and the Men Who Starved for Science*, researchers observed a compromised humanity and a throwback to animal behavior among the men.[12] As participants lost weight and essentially began to starve, not only did they become incredibly and solely focused on food, but their hunger took on epic proportions—participants reported having violent fantasies and contemplating suicide, murder, and ultimately cannibalism. While most

EXPANDING BULIMIA

Today, most people are aware of the definition of bulimia—that it translates to "binge and purge." But what does purge mean, exactly? The most familiar methods of purging include vomiting and laxative use. However, official diagnostic criteria include the following behaviors in the definition of bulimia: use of diuretics, enemas, and excessive exercise.

You need not vomit or use laxatives or diuretics to be diagnosed with bulimia. If you follow binges with periods of fasting and food restriction (*I ate so much—I'm not going to eat for at least a day*), where restricting is used to compensate, you might still meet the criteria.

Remember: eating problems exist along a continuum. The possibility of a nonpurging bulimia adds yet another shade of gray.

self-imposed food restrictors thankfully do not arrive at the point of suicidal or homicidal ideation, what we learned from the Minnesota starvation study is that restriction leads to food preoccupation and when the restriction ends, there is a tendency to overeat (reports of binge eating occurred as the experimental restriction was lifted). The average dieter or restrictive eater may become obsessed with food and will likely overeat when she loosens her restrictions. Strict dieters are likely to consume more food in a select period of time than they would have without the fast, with the additional problem of having toyed (albeit briefly) with their metabolism.

Exercise: Stopping the Diet-Binge Cycle

The easiest way to disrupt the diet-binge cycle is to intervene at the dieting stage. What would it take for you to give up your next diet? The next plan or program that seduces you, the next time you were planning to begin again (Diet Mondays, anyone?), resist the urge by reminding yourself that diets eventually lead to overeating. If you need some convincing, do some research on the efficacy of diets. It's just not worth it. Eat healthfully while allowing yourself what you want. Your relationship with food is sure to improve.

WHAT ABOUT FASTING?

Fasting for health has become all the rage, but as any observer of the Jewish holiday Yom Kippur or the Muslim period of Ramadan may tell you, fasting is a great way to become obsessed with food. It's a unique psychophysiological state in which food often becomes a primary focus, regardless of the intent to focus on religious or spiritual matters. Fasters often report spending a great deal of time during the fast thinking about their hunger and when they'll eat again. Psychologically, when told not to think about a white horse (or a White Castle burger), that's exactly what we can't seem to do.

Fasting can also lead to bingeing. Fasters often overindulge the night before as they stock up for the fast and may similarly overindulge postfast. One of my readers from Saudi Arabia noted that the Ramadan observance, which calls for fasting during sunlight hours, is a "recipe for bingeing at night."

Compulsive Exercising/Exercising as Punishment

Restricting food and the often-inevitable descent into the diet-binge cycle are two ways disordered behavior expresses itself, but there's a third major category: overexercising. For many women, exercise toward the goal of weight maintenance or reduction can become just as compulsive or ritualistic as eating behaviors. Though the actual intensity or duration of the exercise may not necessarily be alarming, the underlying relationship between a woman and her exercise routine can be the giveaway that a problem exists. Whereas a dedicated exerciser may prefer not to skip a workout, a compulsive exerciser will feel that she *can't*. Her concerns about her weight and shape, and the role exercise plays in maintaining her calorie balance, will preoccupy her to the point where her workouts take precedence over other important aspects of her life.[13]

Beth, a 29-year-old woman who jogs for an hour a day, is a good example. Seven days a week, she laces up her running shoes and hits the pavement. On some days, she is tired or busy or has been invited to socialize with friends. Still, her run comes first. Beth doesn't believe she's an overexerciser because her run is just an hour a day and she doesn't add any mileage as a result of occasionally eating more. If she has to miss a run because she's too ill to exercise, she won't consciously cut her food intake. Her run is about fitness, she insists. Running allows her to fight stress and "blow off steam." Friends and family admire Beth's commitment to her health.

Only Beth knows her true motivation for running: to keep her weight down. When she can't run, she becomes anxious that she'll upset the caloric balance she's created. When her husband mentions an upcoming vacation, she worries about having the time and energy to complete her daily ritual. If she misses a run, let alone two or three, she can picture her abdomen extending, her legs widening in girth.

At some point in the future, Beth may be plagued with overuse injuries. She may find that she gets sick a lot. But she will still attempt to run because for her, while exercise is a health-related behavior, it's also unhealthy.

For some women, this drive to exercise goes a step further. Beth did not run extra miles if she ate an extra piece of cake, but many women do. The more they eat, the more they move, in an effort to neutralize excess calories.

Though they may at times feel tired or weak from pushing themselves beyond what their bodies are willing to give, they keep going, because for them, their motivation has morphed from self-care to self-attack.

Unfortunately, sometimes fitness instructors tend to reinforce this mindset. Some encourage their classes to push through a challenging portion to burn off a recent holiday meal. In one yoga class I took, the teacher suggested that an inversion practice can reduce the appearance of cellulite. In another indoor cycling class, the instructor yelled, "Who wants to change your body?" If he meant "change" as in get stronger, faster, and more flexible, I might have joined with the moderate, collective cheer, but I don't think that's what he meant. He repeated the question with more oomph until he got a louder response. The expectation is that, by the very fact that we're exercising, we're unhappy with ourselves.

The more we exercise to lose weight, burn calories or fat, or change ourselves, the more likely we are to push beyond our limits (hour-long inversions, anyone?), turn exercise into punishment, and reduce the joy associated with the inherent act of moving our bodies. It's no wonder that such a large percentage of people who start an exercise program drop out.

But when we exercise to realize the physical and psychological gains associated with movement, for improving our fitness, for empowering us, and even for fun, we can easily sign on for a lifelong commitment. When we so enjoy dancing and hiking and climbing and swimming and cycling and strengthening and stretching, why would we ever stop?

EXERCISE: Rethinking Exercise

Exercise has a wealth of physical and psychological benefits having nothing to do with weight or size management. I've started a list. How many more benefits can you add?

- Improves mood
- Makes me feel accomplished
- Builds strength so I can carry in all the groceries at one time
- Burns off restless energy from an entire workday spent seated in a chair
- Builds camaraderie (on a team or in a class setting)

- Exposes me to fresh air and beautiful views
- Provides me an opportunity to connect to the earth
- Keeps my blood pressure low and my heart in good health
- Creates a portal through which I can practice mindfulness, following both movement and breath

Addicted to Food?

Given the tight hold that food has on us, and the extent to which eating or not eating or exercising or not exercising can run our lives, you might be wondering—is it possible we're addicted to food?

The similarity between a food fixation and addiction is all too clear in the following excerpt from Caroline Knapp's book, *Drinking: A Love Story*, in which she describes and diagnoses alcohol dependence:

> Are you driven by a feeling of hunger and need? When someone sets a bottle of wine on the dinner table, do you find yourself glancing at it subversively, possessively, the way you might look at a lover you long for but don't quite trust? When someone pours you a glass from the bottle, do you take careful note of the level of liquid in the glass, and measure it secretly against the level of liquid in the other glasses, and hold your breath for just a second until you're assured you have enough?[14]

If you substitute "plate of nachos" or "bowl of ice cream" for "bottle of wine," you've just diagnosed an unhealthy relationship with food.

Because I specialize in both eating disorders and addictions, I've spent a lot of time pondering the similarities between the two. There are so many, that sometimes, in my writing and speaking on each topic, my language will involve mere word substitution to convey the difference. Both alcohol/ substance abuse and eating disorders are coping mechanisms that allow us to tolerate difficult emotions and to manage our lives more effectively— until, of course, the coping strategy itself becomes problematic. Both are behavioral addictions designed to ward off distress. Both have genetic and environmental antecedents. Both involve oral fixation (in the case of most substances), which signals, in psychobabble, unmet dependency needs. Both destroy the lives of others and ourselves.

Sabrina's story is a good example. Sabrina began using food to comfort herself when she was a child. After her father died when she was a teenager, she sought to regain control of her life by controlling her eating and exercise. She dropped from 145 pounds (a healthy weight for her height) to an extremely low weight and body fat percentage. "I shut out the real world so that I could maintain this strict, regimented lifestyle," she said. After four years of severe restriction, she sought out nutritional therapy when she was twenty-three. After a year, she began to gain weight.

At that point, she said, "Something just *clicked*, like a switch being shut off.... Something finally gave and like *that* I was bingeing." Sabrina started eating from vending machines, searching for food she hadn't allowed herself to eat for years. Within ten months she gained more than 100 pounds, but she couldn't stop eating. Eventually she was able to return to her starting weight of 145 pounds through rigid dieting throughout the week and "bingeing my brains out on the weekend." She shares, "It is the worst feeling ever to not be able to have just one cookie without it sending me into a total downward spiral of carb-coma madness."

Today Sabrina still struggles with eating some of her trigger foods—like her favorite cereal—without anxiously predicting an addictive response. She tells herself, "I didn't gain 100 pounds from letting myself have a bowl [of cereal]. Who knew? Freedom = an allowed, calmly eaten bowl of Raisin Bran."

Clearly, people can use food in an addictive way. The research, however, is inconclusive regarding whether food itself is addictive. Some studies promote the concept of addiction to certain foods, including sugar, fat, and wheat. Advocates of food addiction argue that consumption of these foods activates brain centers associated with addiction. Opponents argue that we can't be addicted to a substance we need to live (similar to oxygen). The brain research is inconclusive, partly because it's difficult to separate out what might be an actual addiction versus what is a behavioral response to a period of deprivation. In most cases of women who complain of food addiction, they have previously restricted their intake of certain types of foods. When they do allow themselves access to these foods, they overeat or feel out of control. They are finally allowing themselves access to the "forbidden fruit," and it's difficult to manage this access. The permission they've granted themselves to eat this fruit is usually temporary, so there's a sense of getting as much as they can in an allowed window. The subsequent binge is a behavioral response to the deprivation, not a sign of addiction.

That being said, most scientists and doctors can agree that certain highly palatable foods seem to signal continued eating even past fullness or satisfaction. Foods that contain sugar, fat, or salt, or some combination of those three, are often difficult to put down.

While I've yet to see convincing evidence that we can be addicted to food, I do believe we can use food in an addictive way; the subtlety is an important distinction. Unlike alcohol or painkillers, perfect abstinence cannot exist with food. If you become abstinent, you'll die. I've seen, and you've probably seen in your own life, countless examples of how practicing abstinence from certain foods like sugar, white flour, or wheat does nothing to promote a healthy relationship with food; on the contrary, avoiding categories of food typically increases one's symptoms of disordered eating. Some will avoid certain foods for years at a time, reporting that abstinence works for them—until it doesn't.

Not uncommonly, patients will present with both an eating disorder and alcohol/substance abuse. When one remits, the other, sometimes, will worsen. It's not surprising. The bottom line is, we need a way to cope, and when we're robbed of one weapon, we're quick to return to the arsenal to determine what remains. Clearly, people can use food in an addictive way. If you have an addictive relationship with these foods, the best way to learn to handle them is to moderate your intake through exactly that, moderation, rather than abstinence.

EXERCISE: Saying Good-Night to Food

On an episode of *Will & Grace*, Grace and Karen are finishing up a restaurant meal when the leftovers are put into a doggy bag and delivered to their table. Grace exclaims, "Yay! I'm so excited! I can't wait until I'm hungry again!"[15]

If you're enjoying a tasty meal, how difficult is it for you to stop when you're feeling full? It may be challenging to put down your fork because you were taught to clean your plate, because you don't often treat yourself to tasty food, or because it's just that good. The next time this happens, try something new. Stop where you are and promise yourself that you can eat more as soon as you get hungry again (this might mean taking a doggy-bag from a restaurant). Or, promise yourself that you can have this exact same meal again at another time, that this isn't your only opportunity. Even with these promises, pushing your plate away can still be a challenge, sometimes more so at dinnertime, the last meal of the day. Ending a meal is like saying good-bye, in a way. Nutrition therapist Elyse Resch refers to this as "the sadness of saying enough."[16] To ease yourself through the process, have some sort of postmeal ritual—for example, put away your leftovers and have a cup of tea or turn to something enjoyable such as a phone call with a friend or your favorite magazine.

Body Image Behaviors: Checks and Balances

I love the following sentiment by author Geneen Roth:

> Give away the scale and keep your power. You don't need a piece of metal to tell you if you've gained or lost weight. You already know the answer. And you don't need it to tell you whether you're allowed to like yourself today. You are. You belong here. No matter what you weigh, you deserve joy and happiness and connection to people you love.[17]

It's so empowering and true. In this chapter I've mainly been discussing disordered eating behavior and the compensations some women make when they feel they've overeaten. However, another type of disordered behavior exists, one that may be so common you don't realize it's a problem— judging and disliking your body. As I mention throughout this book, body dissatisfaction is rampant in our culture. Ask yourself, how many times a day do you think negative thoughts about the way you look? The answer: thirteen. According to a *Glamour* survey, every day, women of all sizes think cruel or judgmental thoughts about their bodies almost once per waking hour. Experts who spoke to *Glamour* about these results attribute these negative thoughts in part to our celebrity-obsessed culture (see chapter 4), to our habit of denigrating ourselves when we meet up socially ("You look great!" "Are you kidding? I'm so bloated today."), and to our society's pursuit of the perfect body ideal.[18]

Literally weighing oneself against this perfect body ideal can lead to a need to check and judge your body frequently: "How's my weight? My measurements? What about my reflection?" For some women, these checks and balances become highly ritualistic, a way to determine their worth and mood for the rest of the day. For many, the scale becomes the chief offender, the ultimate arbiter of a woman's self-esteem. Says Leslie Goldman, author of *The Locker Room Diaries: The Naked Truth about Women, Body Image, and Re-imagining the "Perfect" Body*, "I remember when I was writing my book, I interviewed a woman who said, 'At 114, I feel skinny and beautiful; at 118, I feel fat.' And this is a smart, educated lawyer.... You can see women get on the scale, and if they're unhappy, they'll slump. They'll take off their flip-flops or towel to try to lose that extra quarter pound."[19]

Does the number on your scale determine how you'll feel the rest of the day? In her TED Talk, "Why It's Okay to Be Fat: A Story of Self-Acceptance," Golda Poretsky refers to this as "scale-dependent self-esteem."[20] What starts out as a regular healthy check-in can quickly take over your life. A good example comes from one of my regular blog readers:

> I weigh myself first thing in the morning, after I go to the bathroom. (This morning it was 3x in a row just to make sure the number was correct.) Then I weigh myself when I get home from the gym and many times throughout the day. After I eat, before and after I pee, at night. Lots of times I step on the scale a few times to make sure the number's right. The thoughts and feelings that occur are different. Sometimes it's a feeling of relief because I didn't gain weight. Other times it's anger and disgust because I gained a pound. Sometimes it's fear because I'm afraid I won't be able to stop this behavior (losing weight), other times it's happiness because the number is going down...I get very anxious when I can't weigh myself because I'm afraid I have gained a ton of weight. Being away from my scale is not fun! It would probably be very freeing to stop but I can't do that.

What starts out as a daily checking in can quickly become compulsive. One of my blog readers wrote that she used to be religious about her daily weigh-ins because "it kept me accountable." At a certain point, you may want to ask yourself—accountable to what, exactly?

I've never owned a scale myself. In my practice, I've worked with women who weigh themselves more than one hundred times a week. I always encourage them to stop. I know it may sound radical to you, but imagine freeing yourself of that daily judgment. It may be easier than you think. One of my blog readers who tossed out her scale found it challenging to "break the scale ritual" but ultimately avoided weighing herself for months "without feeling even slightly tempted."

Of course, scales are not the only ways in which we measure our bodies. Frequent mirror checking is another common behavior, along with an overreliance on how clothes fit. Often women who succeed in tossing their scales simply swap in another behavior that's just as detrimental to their self-esteem. Even respected author and speaker Geneen Roth, the woman responsible for the empowering quote at the beginning of this section, encourages a substitute metric: "Try something radical. Instead of trusting your scale, trust your jeans—they never lie."[21]

Have you ever heard a woman say, "Oh, I don't weigh myself; I just go by how my clothes fit"? At first this comment may sound confident, until you examine what she's really saying. She doesn't measure herself by the scale—but what happens when her jeans get too tight? Even relying on clothes can become compulsive. I've known women who, fearing they've gained weight, decide to break out several pairs of pants that they believe will tell the truth. One of my blog readers wrote that her two favorite pairs of dress pants were her most reliable test. Another reader added that as much as she hated using her clothes to determine her self-worth or need to diet, she's had this "way of thinking for a long time."

Judging oneself by a reflection is another common ritual. I've worked with a number of women who detail stories of obsessive mirror checking. For many, they will abuse any opportunity at catching a reflection, whether it be in a store window or sunny sidewalk silhouette. They'll scan their images for shape, fat, muscle, bones, and any other indication of increase or decrease. Fitting rooms, with their notoriously unflattering lighting, are particularly challenging for many women; one of my blog readers stated that a recent fitting room experience made her feel like she must "work out that instant."

You can probably relate to this feeling; many of us can. A few years back, I encountered a woman in her early twenties trying on a pair of skinny jeans in a communal dressing room. She called to her friend outside, "The jeans aren't working." I liked the jeans, so I said simply, "They look nice."

"Yeah, but I have runner's thighs," she responded.

"Uh-huh."

"And this makes them look worse."

She looked at me, expecting a reaction. After debating with myself about whether to answer as just Stacey or Dr. Stacey, therapist, I responded, "Well, I'm actually a psychologist and quite interested in body image, so I'm not going to agree with you on that one."

We had a laugh and exchanged names. Then she called in her friend to join us.

"See, don't they look awful?" the jeans-wearer asked her friend. Even in the presence of a body image therapist, she was unable to disbelieve what she felt the mirror was telling her about her body.

The three of us commented on the psychology of the communal dressing room experience. "I probably should just have a seat and set up shop," I joked.

"Yeah, do you have a card? I'm kinda serious here. It's probably something I should look into."

Mirror checking can have a strong hold even when we know rationally that it's not helpful. As one of my blog readers noted, even assessing herself naked in a full-length mirror isn't particularly useful. "It's hard to tell if I've gotten bigger or smaller!" If the metric isn't helpful, why continue to use it? Why measure yourself at all? A new and somewhat controversial trend in body image issues is mirror fasting—avoiding one's reflection as a way to improve body image. According to Dr. Vivian Diller in *Psychology Today*, total abstention from addictive behaviors like mirror checking, weighing oneself, or trying on skinny pants is not realistic or necessarily helpful in the long run. "So while we can take a break from actual mirrors that surround us as adults—to help think about why and how we rely on them—it's the adjustments we make to our own, internal view of ourselves that are necessary," she says.[22]

I agree. Eventually, you should aim to be comfortable with yourself to the point where seeing your reflection in passing or being weighed at the doctor's office won't ruin your day. But in the short-term, experimenting with stopping the body image checks and balances can be an enlightening and freeing exercise. One of my blog readers summed it up best, noting how much better she felt once she tossed her scale and her clothing size assessments. "I'm just more comfortable being me."

ASSIGNMENT: Ending the Trifecta

Weighing. Mirror glancing. Checking the fit of our clothes. I call this the self-esteem trifecta. How often do you weigh yourself? How about checking yourself in the mirror or the fit of your clothing? What types of thoughts and feelings precipitate these behaviors? How do you feel after each behavior? What would it be like to stop? If stopping is too challenging, could you cut down gradually on these behaviors?

Conclusion

Our culture encourages an emotional attachment to food ("American as apple pie") and in many ways sets us up to fail daily in our resolve to eat only when we're hungry. In addition to being surrounded by surplus, we're bombarded by the influences of thriving food and diet industries, which inundate us with potentially harmful messages—"indulge but pay for it later." Is it any wonder that we have developed so many disordered approaches to eating, exercise, and thinking about our bodies?

In the next chapter, I look in greater detail at some of the messages that reinforce our disordered behaviors on a daily basis.

CHAPTER 3

⫻ Toxic Language

Because even the smallest of words
can be the ones to hurt you, or save you.
— NATSUKI TAKAYA

ONCE, I VISITED SOME FRIENDS FOR BRUNCH. On their kitchen counter, they displayed a baby picture of their niece. Another guest, gazing upon it, commented on how chubby the girl had been as a baby. I heard her use the words "fat baby," "not a cute baby," and "It's a good thing she turned out cute." Half an hour later, the same guest spoke about her own young daughter. "Would you believe that she's only six, and she already won't wear one of her coats because it makes her look fat? I don't know where she gets that from."

Well, I do. Her daughter may have come by her weight consciousness from the myriad television, magazine, and Internet advertisements surrounding her, or from the crystal-clear references to the discrepant value of fat and thin in books, movies, and on television. Or maybe she acquired it from the glory and praise that slender women receive in the media, in the workplace, and around town just for being thin. Perhaps she learned the thinner-is-better message from the pity and scorn assigned to those who are fat, or simply not thin. If she didn't pick up her fear of fat from any of those sources, I'd guess she got the message from her mother and from all of us—from subtle, often unknowing, communications in the home and in the world outside that began, gradually, to eat away at her developing sense of self.

You may think that I have a biased view of the world because I work with women with disordered eating and write a popular blog on the subject. However, it's not just the women I see in my practice and hear from online who've helped me form the hypothesis of this book. Being out in the world and interacting with others, overhearing everyday conversations, and consuming media myself have all convinced me that nearly every woman is susceptible to body image issues and a disordered relationship with food. Though we may think we're not talking about our bodies in a negative way, the toxic language of weight and body shape concerns has become so commonplace in our everyday conversations, our advertising, and our popular culture that we fail to even notice it, never mind challenge it. Unlike other psychiatric diagnoses, disordered eating is actively encouraged and promoted in our culture, fueled in part by its own burgeoning language. Once you start noticing this language and how almost everything in Western culture can be discussed in terms of weight, you'll begin to see the depths of how eating disordered our culture is and how these messages, both by us and for us, sustain not just a diet industry, but also a collective neurosis that gathers momentum at every turn.

In this chapter, I'll be looking at how this toxic language surrounds us, starting with advertising, entertainment, and the Internet and culminating in the everyday conversations we're having with one another and with the children in our lives.

Advertising

"Everybody wants to lose weight…but which 'diet pill' is right for you?"[1] So reads one print ad featuring a near-naked, frustrated-looking woman crouched upon a scale. Everyone wants to lose weight, we're told. There is zero room for conversation on the subject.

Advertising like this is one of the most blatant and pervasive promoters of body dissatisfaction in our culture, and we can't escape it; ads appear on television and billboards, in magazines, along the side of Facebook pages and websites, and before the movie trailers at the theater. Even when an advertisement is not actively promoting beauty products, fashion, or the latest diet, it's reflecting societal perceptions of women's bodies. Thin, hourglass-shaped bodies are used to sell everything from fragrances to eyeglasses, from beer to car insurance. They also sell us ourselves—not as we are, but rather, an idealized, perfected version we're longing to achieve.

Jean Kilbourne, an expert on the harmful and powerful nature of advertising, says this:

> To a great extent, advertising tells us who we are and who we should be. What does advertising tell us today about women? It tells us, just as it did 10 and 20 and 30 years ago, that what's most important about women is how we look.[2]

Capitalizing on our worst fears (gaining weight) and our biggest dreams (losing it), ads reflect and fuel our collective drive toward thinness. A population of women who desire to be thin and beautiful and flawless but who may never reach that goal is good for the economy. This ethos is so central to the advertising industry that even ads that are not, at first glance, about our bodies invoke the "weight card" to sell their products. For example, one print ad for Cotton Incorporated says, "Nothing complements imperfect genes like the perfect jeans."[3] At the birth of a baby, most parents will be relieved when genetic disorders, congenital conditions, and other issues resulting from problem genes are ruled out. If the baby has all his or her reflexes and ten fingers and toes, the child is perfect. So, why are a few extra pounds considered a genetic problem later on? The answer is unclear, but apparently the right jeans are the solution.

Like this ad, many directly target women's fears about being too big, offering their products as the solutions to our war against weight. In 2006, a post–New Year's Special K advertorial, "Weightless: A Short Story," introduced readers to Melissa—a woman who yearned for German chocolate cake but instead chose to "indulge in a Special K chocolatey [sic] drizzle bar." I wouldn't exactly call a low-fat snack indulging, but maybe I missed the point. Thankfully, the writer instructs me, "Every great story contains great conflict. A moment when the hero fights her greatest enemy and remains true, or all is lost." Had the story continued along this train of thought, I'm sure it would have highlighted the good versus evil, yin versus yang, German chocolate cake versus Special K drizzle bar duality that we encounter on a daily basis. At the end of the tale, Melissa finally weighed herself after two weeks of "indulging" on drizzle bars. "For a second she thought she couldn't look as the little dial spun toward a number. It stopped. She was almost a full six pounds lighter! She wanted to jump for joy. This was going to be a very good day! This was going to be the start of something great."[4] Never mind that Melissa might not have energy to jump at all, given the fact that she'd been eating a small bowl of cereal for two-thirds of her meals, or that her weight loss could be water weight and she'd probably gain it back (and then some, as you learned in chapter 2). For now, she'd reached her primary goal: to get thinner.

Yoplait Light yogurt shared a similar ad on television, featuring a swimsuit-clad woman shimmying around a boardwalk at the beach, her body covered with an inflatable raft. When she finally removes it, we see this millennium's version of the "Itsy Bitsy Teenie Weenie Yellow Polka Dot Bikini."[5] Yoplait Light is the "weight-loss boost" that gave our heroine the courage to perform this particular raft-ectomy. The primary purpose of the ad is to market the diet-friendly aspects of dairy, but the underlying message is that body acceptance will only occur if you're thin. If you're not, you'd better re-raft-wrap yourself.

Cosmetics also tie their advertising to our fear of fat and our shame at having it. Cosmetics giant Sephora carries a product called fatgirlslim. "This lean, mean circulation stimulating, slimming cream with caffeine and QuSomes (a proprietary delivery enhancer that helps penetration) helps smooth the skin as it firms, trims, tones, and energizes."[6] By buying fatgirlslim, you're not just fighting the war on fat—you're admitting to the Sephora staff, yourself, and anyone who visits your bathroom that you could be fat (but thankfully, you're doing something about it).

But what if we apply the cream and eat the cereal bars and yogurt cups but are still hungry? An advertisement for Slim-Fast Optima Shakes suggests that its product "controls hunger for up to four hours,"[7] a substantial duration in our crusade. We forget to consider that hunger might serve a biological (and psychological) function. Imagine if other products were designed to help us gain control over physiological processes: an oxygenated air freshener to help you avoid breathing for up to a minute or a specially formulated beverage allowing you to delay urination. Why aren't these products on the market? We purchase products such as Slim-Fast because we learn from a very young age the falsehood that hunger is controllable and that we need an ally to help us wage the war against it.

Madison Avenue knows that self-accepting women are poor consumers. Advertisers may even purposely target women on days and times we feel our least attractive. One marketing survey in 2013 "was designed to identify when women feel most vulnerable about their appearance throughout the week in order to determine the best timing for beauty product messages and promotions."[8]

And if a product can make you feel ugly, insecure, and lacking (i.e., accomplish the same work as most diet plans, women's magazines, and the entire spring line of New York City's Fashion Week), it's sure to sell. The more advertising can undermine your self-worth, the more likely you are to fall for the product's weight-loss gimmicks. Slink brand jeans are a perfect example. Slink jeans run about three sizes too small. One of my friends typically wears a size 4/6. When she tried on a Slink size 10, the pants were too tight. What seems at first like a faulty marketing plan (we all know women *love* to buy clothes a size smaller than they usually are, hence the proliferation of vanity sizing) is, perhaps, marketing genius. To exclude even thin women places the Slink brand in a prized, elusive category meant only for a select skinny few.

With so many not-so-subtle advertising messages targeting women and their bodies, is there any accountability in advertising? The National Eating Disorders Association's (NEDA's) Media Watchdog program targets advertising that portrays unhealthy messages about body shape and size with the understanding that such messages may contribute to the incidence of eating disorders.

In 2002, I learned of and became involved in NEDA's media program. One of my first tasks was to meet with female students at a local university to get their feedback on a particular ad—a promotion for Nutri-Grain breakfast

ISRAEL GETS REAL WITH ADVERTISING

In 2013, Israel passed a revolutionary law: advertisers can no longer use underweight models (those with a body mass index, or BMI, under 18.5), and images that have been airbrushed to make models appear thinner must be labeled.[9] What effect do you think this new law will have? Will it help?

bars. The ad featured a slim, attractive woman with two cinnamon buns affixed to her rear end. Aside from the obvious untruth that promotes our culture's widespread craze for spot reduction (cinnamon buns don't land directly on your buns), what struck me and the students most was the ad's copy: "Respect yourself in the morning."[10] Eating a Nutri-Grain breakfast bar would allow you to maintain your self-respect, whereas eating a cinnamon bun (or two) was akin to engaging in an unplanned, unladylike, orgiastic feast. Breakfast bar or cinnamon bun? Madonna or whore? You make the call.

This juxtaposition of food, morality, and sex that's sold to us in product ads seems to play out in our private thoughts and conversations, too. (More about this in "A Tongue of Weight," on page 48.) Advertising would have us believe that moral behavior has nothing to do with our character or our behavioral transgressions but everything to do with what we allow to pass beyond our lips. Today's woman of virtue wears white, borders on too thin, and avoids carbohydrates at all costs. She flirts with temptation in the form of a fat-free, sugar-free frozen dessert, but when she reaches for a handful of M&Ms toppings, she may hear an imaginary soundtrack better suited to stealing or deceiving or sleeping with a married man: musician Chris Isaak's song "Baby Did a Bad Bad Thing." (One diet ad begs, "Feel good about cheating.")[11]

In his book *The Diet Myth: Why America's Obsession with Weight Is Hazardous to Your Health*, Paul Campos writes about our moralization of eating and not eating:

> Our current obsession with maintaining an absurdly thin body has more to do with darker strains in the American character—with that part of American culture that has

always distrusted desire in general, and has now come to
fear food in particular, as a harbinger of sloth, gluttony,
lust, and every other deadly consequence of uncontrolled
indulgence in life's pleasures.[12]

Food we enjoy is often thought of as a guilty pleasure. Think about how
a restaurant menu might describe its celebrated soufflé: decadent, sinful. Even
the word itself, "soufflé," sounds a bit flirty. We describe food as "lustful,"
indulgence as "gluttonous," and the result of enjoying too much as "sloth."
I wouldn't be surprised if we could fit "envy" and "greed" into the equation,
too. What might be the penance for the Seven Deadly Sins of Eating? Perhaps
the Seven Heavenly Virtues of Dieting. Number one might be "abstinence
against gluttony," which, taken to the extreme, looks a lot like anorexia.

The messages we receive about food and eating contain a constant push
and pull. On the one hand, we're seduced by statements like "Ice cream
is meant to be an indulgence" (spotted at a Dairy Queen store) and by
foods described to be "decadent," "luscious," and "mouth watering."[13] On
the other, we're advised to "control our hunger" and "watch our weight."
Most confusing of all are the advertisements that beckon us to "Eat all you
want and still lose weight," the conceptual holy grail of the dieting world.[14]
These mixed messages, in concert with other triggers, can propel an already
vulnerable individual to toy with bingeing and purging—how else might she
partake in the sensual pleasures of food while still dancing with perfection?

EXERCISE: A Critical Eye on Ads

Spend a day with a critical eye for advertising related to weight. Where
do you encounter these ads? See how often they pop up, not just while
you are reading magazines or watching television, but also on your bus
or subway platform, on billboards at the side of the road, and within your
social media account. When you come across each ad, ask yourself, how
does the ad represent women? What does the product/plan/food/clothing
promise? How do you feel when looking at or listening to the ad?

The Joke's on Me (Or, "Entertainment Thinks Eating Disorders Are Funny")

If advertising sells unhealthy approaches to eating and body image, entertainment may be even worse—because it takes eating disorders lightly, making real illnesses fodder for comedians. On one episode of the animated sitcom *Family Guy*, for example, a high school cheerleader says to another, "Wow, it sure is great being thin and popular. Let's go throw up."[15] Apparently, bulimia makes for good humor. The joke continues on E!'s *101 Incredible Celebrity Slimdowns*, when a comedian shares, with a wink-wink, "When I know I'm going to have to wear a bikini, I usually throw up everything I eat for about a week straight."[16] Even in its sarcasm, her message condones a bulimic behavior and simultaneously minimizes the psychic pain of those actually struggling with the disease. (Though perhaps she does really purge— in which case, she doesn't take her own problem seriously.) In passing, I once saw a TV host quip, "Bulimia isn't a disease; it's a decision." He was wrong, of course, and his comment diminished the severity of a psychiatric disorder while promoting an inaccurate, just-snap-out-of-it mentality. Messages like these, couched in humor, erroneously convince the public that people can casually dabble in eating disordered behaviors and then resume normalcy at will.

Anorexia is another popular target for jokes. A T-shirt that once made the Internet rounds, modeled by a clearly obese male, reads, "I Beat Anorexia." Is this funny? Never mind that this man could be suffering from a condition related to obesity, or that he could have an eating disorder of his own, like binge-eating disorder or OSFED. Forget about him for a moment and imagine other variations on this joke: a smiling, well-rested woman wearing an "I Beat Depression" T-shirt or a healthy-weight male with infection-free skin wearing "I Beat HIV." Neither of those scenarios is amusing. We take depression and HIV seriously—why not eating disorders? How did the psychiatric diagnoses with the highest rates of mortality become convenient material for jokes? One of my blog readers contributed an interesting insight on the subject. Her point was that we admire thinness in celebrities and those around us and feel that being thin will bring us happiness, respect, and praise. It's no wonder, she reasoned, that we might joke around about disordered eating—"It's so desirable and worthy!"

Reflecting this perceived desirability or even trendiness are the dismissive new words entering our vernacular—cutesy bastardizations of the word "anorexia" that minimize the gravity of an actual eating disorder diagnosis. *Urban Dictionary* defines "blondorexia" as a condition plaguing those who have "the inability to see the true color of their hair. They will often bleach it to the point where it becomes frizzy and breaks off, and still not be satisfied."[17] A related word, "tanorexia," describes the state of having gone overboard in the tanning salon, resulting in that telltale, faux orange glow. "Drunkorexia" refers to the collegiate trick of restricting food in anticipation of a night out drinking. Then there's "manorexia." I first heard this term years ago in an episode of E!'s *50 Most Shocking Celebrity Confessions*. The subject: How Dennis Quaid developed an eating problem after losing 40 pounds for the role of Doc Holliday in *Wyatt Earp*.[18] "Manorexia" is a misnomer, incidentally; a separate distinction is unnecessary to identify the minority (but growing) percentage of eating disorder sufferers who happen to be male[19] (including Quaid himself, who has admitted to struggling with anorexia).[20]

Unfortunately, these jokes and casual mentions of eating disorders have become so common that people are starting to believe that disordered behavior is no big deal. While writing this book in a café, I overheard a man tell his friend, "I'm on a diet. My goal weight is 4 pounds." When I turned around to tell him I was writing a book on eating disorders, he laughed and said, "My whole life, I've wanted to be anorexic—but I'm always hungry. I wish I were anorexic."

"No, you don't," I rejoined.

"Yes, I do—my sister was anorexic. I was so jealous." I stared. "I'm just kidding," he said. "I joke a lot."

Sadly, even people who should know better have a tendency to make light of disordered behavior. An ophthalmologist once told me, "It would be kind of nice to have an eating disorder for a little while, lose 30 pounds, and then get rid of it." As a medical doctor, he would never suggest he'd like to dabble in opioid addiction. No one jokes about how appealing a stint of schizophrenia would be or how nice it would be to have a panic attack now and then. A blog reader pointed out that cancer also leads to rapid weight loss and wondered whether these individuals "ever wish they had cancer."

When people joke about wishing they had anorexia or bulimia, they're missing the point: they've internalized our warped societal views around food and weight—which, coupled with the right predisposition, could lead someone down the road to a disorder—and that road is not funny, nor easy to exit for those who are on it. Another of my blog readers shared from her own experience that people had sometimes approached her, too, and told her they wished they could develop an eating disorder. This caused her to reflect on her all-consuming and dangerous behaviors and prompted her to want to ask them if they, too, were interested in holding on to "life by a thread."

EXERCISE: Beeping Body Image Talk

My college roommate studied education. She pointed out to her friends that using the r-word carelessly (e.g., "That guy I met the other night was so retarded!") was both a misuse of the word and insensitive to people with developmental disabilities. Every time she heard one of us use it without thinking, she'd interrupt with a loud "Beep!" It worked. After a while, we'd hear the "beep" before saying the word and we'd stop ourselves. Eventually, we stopped saying it and even thinking it.

For one week, try "beeping" silently whenever you hear a joke about eating disorders, or any sort of body image conversation or body talk at all. If you're like me, you may find you soon sound like a semitruck in reverse.

The Internet and the Pro-Ana Community

A few months after starting the blog that was the genesis for this book, I saw my traffic grow to the point where I got curious about my readership. How were all these visitors finding me? In an effort to find out, I decided to track the search engine queries that brought people to the site. The results were not exactly heartening. Many of the search queries were related to celebrity dress sizes, diet, and weight concerns: "Is Mandy Moore getting fat?," "Beyoncé Knowles's recent weight-loss secret," and, "Katie Couric's fat arms." Other searches focused on dieting and eating disorder tips and techniques, including advice about "nonpurging bulimia," "starve and barf," and "how to hide an eating disorder."

If web searches speak to our secret curiosities, we seem, overall, to be fascinated with anorexia and the disappearance of flesh. Some of the stranger web queries that brought people to my site: "anorexic 75-lb woman," "Freudian anorexic pregnancy," "ballerina anorexic images," "47-pound anorexic ballerina," and, frustratingly, "anorexic role models."

The most harrowing query to date? "How little can a woman weigh and still live?"

I can't even count the number of searches for *pro-ana* material. If you're not familiar with the concept, pro-ana, or pro-anorexic, websites are designed to provide support for those with eating disorders. Support, in this context, is not what you might expect. The sites describe anorexia (cleverly referred to as "Ana") and bulimia ("Mia") as "lifestyle choices," not diseases, and do not encourage recovery from these conditions. Pro-ana sites anthropomorphize eating disorders, turning serious illnesses into catchy names that sound more like friends you'd meet for lunch than serious physical and psychological illnesses.

Here's an introduction to one site I found in my research but which is no longer online:

> Pro-ana is a source of support for those who are living
> with an eating disorder. Please leave if you are not living
> with anorexia or bulimia, or if you are trying to recover.[21]

Many pro-ana and pro-mia sites glorify starvation, offer encouragement for food restriction, and share tips for easier purging and for hiding one's disorder from others. Message board users offer adulation to those able to toe the fine line between life and death. Some sites even sell red string bracelets (like the Kabbalah bracelets worn by celebrities) to help distinguish those who are pro-ana and pro-mia from the rest of the world.

Some of the most blatant examples of eating disordered language exist in the online forums hosted by these sites. Users share inspiration in the form of pithy quotes ("Nothing tastes as good as thin feels") and pictures of eating disordered or significantly underweight celebrities (filed under "thinspiration"). One site warns its readers not to eat, urging, "Pinch your thigh and see how you don't need food, because you should be eating your own flesh all away from the inside first before you are deserving of actual legitimate sustenance." The same site also encourages eating disorder sufferers to "Remember, think thin, and try not to faint too often or die."[22]

Many in the psychological community, particularly those who serve the eating disorder population, are, as you'd imagine, up in arms by the proliferation of these sites. However, the question of what to do remains an issue. While some Internet hosts have allegedly banned pro-ana sites from their servers, many hosts do not have such a policy. Those who struggle with eating disorders are easily able to find these websites, regardless of any bans.

A young woman I know—I'll call her Juliet—is a good example. Juliet had been wanting to lose weight for a long time and she finally decided to buckle down. Recently, she'd seen a picture of herself and found the image to be completely unacceptable. Juliet knew she wasn't heavy, but she also knew she could easily stand to lose 10 pounds. So, one afternoon, convinced that she was going to finally lose this stubborn weight that seemed to follow her wherever she went, Juliet Googled, "How do you become anorexic?" It wasn't that Juliet really wanted to develop the disorder, but she wanted to know some tricks of the trade. She had always wondered how those with anorexia seemed to have such remarkable willpower. Were there any techniques

IS "FIT" THE NEW "THIN"?

Following in the footsteps of thinspiration is fitspiration (nicknamed "fitspo"): Internet images and slogans designed to motivate us toward our fitness goals. You'll see on social media sites images of women with toned, muscular bodies—especially chiseled abs—accompanied by inspirational messages evoking themes of discipline, failure, and pain. Writer Charlotte Andersen, author of *The Great Fitness Experiment*, points out that, "fitspo may be thinspo in a sports bra. After all, the problem with thinspo is that the images represent a mostly unattainable ideal that requires great sacrifices (both physical and mental) to achieve and I daresay that most of those 'perfect' female bodies, albeit muscular instead of bony, are equally as problematic."[23]

that made it easier? The result of her search loaded on her screen, and she hurriedly read through the first page of hits.

While Juliet had felt she was doing a good job with limiting fats and carbs, she realized now that her efforts were only minimal; these things needed to be removed entirely from her diet! In fact, she learned that she really could eat only a few safe foods—some vegetables, maybe a serving of protein, and fruit if she felt the need for somthing sweet. Her calorie count was too high, too. She needed to cut her daily calorie intake in half. She learned how to feel full on less food by drinking water and lots of coffee.

The pro-ana sites caused Juliet to take her dieting to new extremes. She realized also that she needed to overhaul her exercise efforts. Most of the girls online were consuming very low-calorie diets yet still exercising a lot. Juliet struggled with that, as it was hard to find time and energy to work out, and she barely had any reserves, now that she was eating less food. But she realized this was what had to be done. She had found the manual for weight loss and had to abide by its dictates.

Whether or not pro-ana sites continue to flourish, other media give attention and widespread exposure to the incredible shrinking woman. In one issue of *Star* magazine (available at grocery checkout lines everywhere), I spotted a story entitled, "Skinny S.O.S.! Stars' Scary New Affliction— Foodophobia and It's Contagious!"[24] Though the headline feigned concern, the two-page spread was full of photos of too-thin celebrities. By sharing these images of famous and beloved (but too-thin) stars, the magazine tacitly reinforced these women's unhealthy eating patterns and sizes. Perhaps the only difference between a pro-ana website and a fashion/celebrity magazine is that the website is willing to admit what it is up to.

Similar to pro-ana sites are the seemingly endless number of weight-loss blogs chronicling women's quests to take off pounds. Weight-loss bloggers commonly share the results of their weekly or daily weigh-ins, along with their daily food intake—by meal, food type, and caloric and nutritional content. They congratulate one another when they lose weight and they share tips for losing more. At first glance, their community of interlinked blogs may seem healthy, like a support group for people trying to become more fit.

However, several of these bloggers' diet tips, such as "Drink as much water as possible," show up on pro-ana sites, as well. Weight loss blogs may seem to be about health, but if they're providing similar advice to pro-ana sites, how much of a difference is there between the two? The similarity highlights the slippery slope between ordinary, run-of-the-mill dieting and the type of restriction that could herald an eating disorder.

A Tongue of Weight

"Daily, I put on display for our daughters my intense body dissatisfaction, dieting and perpetual lack of self-confidence," says Doris Smeltzer in her poignant memoir, *Andrea's Voice*. "Did I think they could not hear?"[25] Smeltzer lost her 19-year-old daughter, Andrea, to bulimia in 2002.

Eating disorders can be fatal. Though most people exposed to our culture's toxic language about weight and size will not go on to develop a serious eating disorder, some will—which is why we all need to be aware of how our culture and our everyday language contribute to the problem. What we think and say about our own bodies—and others'—hurts every woman.

The first step in changing how we speak is to develop awareness. The language of body dissatisfaction and thinness worship is a part of our everyday vernacular, part of everything we do—even in contexts where body size is

SHOULD WE BAN PRO-ANA WEBSITES?

Many professionals and parents have made efforts to ban Internet pro-ana sites. The argument is that these sites normalize and promote disordered behavior. (Teens may even pick up more tricks of the trade from these sites.) Pro-ana sites, they point out, can attract young, impressionable girls and wrongly communicate that eating disorders are choices rather than disorders.

Others feel that the sites shouldn't be banned because the suggestions they contain are not so different from those on weight-loss sites and the images they feature are similar to those in fashion magazines. They argue that sites will pop up despite bans; banning them merely robs sufferers of a community of stigma-free support. Instead of banning these sites, they feel we should promote prorecovery sites as an alternative. What do you think?

irrelevant. Flipping through New York City's Zagat's restaurant guide, for example, might yield a description like, "The lounge-like step-out-onto-the-beach décor furthers the fun vibe, as do the cute, pencil-thin staffers, even though service can be iffy."[26] Pencil-thin staffers. Why, of all possible features attributed to a restaurant, must we focus on the size of the servers?

Think, too, about how we automatically tap into our weight-loss obsession in everyday encounters with food and exercise. If you're eating or drinking something delicious—let's say an iced mocha from a café—how often will a friend say something like, "I hate to mention the amount of calories in that"? So much for enjoying your drink; now you're feeling guilty (or feeling bad because you *hadn't* felt guilty). Or maybe you've returned home sweaty after running a few miles at the gym. You're proud of yourself, at how strong you are, at how fast you ran until someone says, "Wow! If you keep that up, you'll lose lots of weight!" So much for appreciating your strength, speed, and how great you feel after a run. Now you may be thinking, "Am I fat?"

We spend too much time thinking and talking about weight, body size, and calorie counts, and the comments we make and the words we use reflect our obsession. We portray hunger, for example, as a demon that must be slain. If we can't kill it, we're encouraged to "reduce," "curb," and "control" it. Never mind that hunger is a necessary signal reminding us to fuel our bodies—we must fight against it. We join the ranks of the "war on fat" as we attempt to "combat cravings" and fight the "battle of the bulge." We enroll in "boot camp" classes and kick off a diet as if we're being stationed overseas. "Sorry, friends, I won't be able to join you for dim sum this week—I'm being shipped out on Monday." A summertime window ad for a women's-only gym features the battle cry "You versus the bikini—let the games begin!" We soldier on, sticking to a diet or fitness "regime" as if it's a plan of attack, avoiding the enemy shrapnel of a whiff of cinnamon sugar from a local bakery or the trace of buttered popcorn at the local cineplex.

The way we describe ourselves is perhaps even worse than the way we describe our hunger. Consider "problem areas." Thanks to product advertisements and women's magazines, you're probably visually or mentally imagining yours right now: stomach, thighs, backs of your arms. Why are these areas problematic? Because they don't appear as we think they should.

We refer to these problem areas, also known as flaws, with kitschy, humorous names, suggesting we're more accepting of them than we really are: saddle bags, spare tires, love handles, double chins, cankles. All these expressions connote excess, parts of our frames that simply shouldn't be. What can we do about them? "Trim," "tighten," and "burn" away that excess flesh.

I find two other body-centered phrases in our diet vernacular particularly irksome. The first is, "She let herself go." She did? Where'd she go? How's the weather out there? The second has a more positive connotation, typically reserved for postdiet or postpregnancy changes: "She got her body back." Wait, where was her body? Was there a ransom involved for its return?

Perhaps one of the most common and maybe more damaging references in our food and body lingo is the distinction between good and bad. You hear these conversations daily:

"I'm going to the gym."

"Oh, you're so good."

Maybe you're not so good. Maybe you're not even "being good." What you're doing, at best, is something that will make you *feel* good, but it has absolutely nothing to do with your behavior, your character, or who you are. One of my blog readers commented on the absurdity of tying eating and exercise choices to character, noting that a family member had once called her "virtuous" for passing on dessert. Truth was, she just isn't a sugar person. But with this preference came accolades for her honor.

Far too often, we're confronted with "good" and "bad." "I had a good day." "I was bad." The truth is, there is no good and bad—the terms are relative. When someone says to me, "I was good," I'll ask her what that means because my definition of good is not necessarily hers. For some women who struggle with eating disorders, for example, restriction is good, but it's not good for me. Good and bad are arbitrary distinctions designed to make us *feel* good or bad. I might argue that every action we take, every relationship we have, and every morsel of food we eat contains both good and bad. "Healthy" and "unhealthy" are unnecessarily categorical, too. As soon as there's a good, there's a bad, and that sets us up for the moralization of food.

The vocabulary we use to describe our bodies and food can affect our interpersonal relationships, too. As women, our body-centered conversations

> **NO BAD FOODS**
>
> Do you find yourself putting food into "good" and "bad" categories? By dichotomizing nutrition like this, you may be moralizing your food choices. For some people, this sorting process can contribute to disordered eating. While I'm not suggesting everyone eat fried food at every meal, to maintain a healthy relationship with food, your choices should reflect the variety of your cravings. Is there a food you crave that you can stop calling "bad" and let yourself enjoy on occasion?

have taken on a language of their own, one we use too often. Novelist and eating disorder survivor Jessica Weiner, in her book *Do I Look Fat in This? (Life Doesn't Begin Five Pounds from Now)*, tackles this issue head-on, speaking of the "Language of Fat." Weiner writes, "In our desperation to engage in the Language of Fat, we use the phrase, 'Do I look fat in this?' as a greeting, a question, a salutation, and a general tribal warrior cry to other women when we are looking for bonding and support."[27]

She goes a step further by examining the frequent lament "I feel fat." She decries, "Fat is not a feeling!"[28] She's right. The basic six human emotions, experienced across all cultures, are happiness, sadness, anger, disgust, surprise, and fear. Nowhere in the body of psychological research is fat a feeling. And yet we all know how fat "feels," and we are more than apt to convey it regularly. "I feel fat," one woman will say to another, and the answer will likely be either, "Oh, you look fine" (with a tacit understanding of how she feels), or, "Yeah, me too." Either way, the women will have bonded, joined by their dissatisfaction with themselves. In today's culture, women commenting on one another's bodies is almost as natural as asking, "How are you?"

Another variation on the "I feel fat" conversation, reserved for reunions after a lapse in contact, is, "You look great!"

"So do you!"

Henceforth, the greeting is complete. The women have exchanged appearance-focused compliments and have established a competitive cease-fire. Only now can they begin to communicate. I decided a while back that I didn't so much like this game. I now make a pointed effort not to focus on others' appearances, and I quickly change the subject when a friend voices her obligatory praise. "Thanks. How have you been doing?" Still, the focus on appearance persists. Once, after sending out a professional update, friends wrote back to me (regarding my accompanying photo), "You look really pretty." Now, it's not that I don't like to hear that, but how about the fact that I've announced a professional accomplishment? As women, is "pretty" the greatest compliment we can give one another?

EXERCISE: Is "Pretty" the Greatest Compliment We Can Give?

For the next week, practice giving compliments to others that aren't based on appearance. Try not to talk about clothes, shoes, hair, or weight. It's difficult, isn't it? Here are some suggested replacement topics. Tell a friend you like the way she expressed a feeling. Comment on her vocabulary. Compliment her on how she manages at home or work. Tell her you enjoy spending time with her. If you feel inspired, you can pledge to stop talking and thinking about yourself (and others) as fat by signing up to participate in Delta Delta Delta's annual Fat Talk Free Week: http://bi3d.tridelta.org/Pledge.

Although "beeping" body image jokes and conversations is a start, to really change things, we need to go further. Let's learn to rewrite the talk that's harming us. The best way to start is to practice by listening to everyday dialogue happening around you. I tried this once while standing in a restaurant entrance waiting for my party to join me for dinner. I overheard two women have the following exchange:

"Can we get spinach dip?"

"Yes! I've been really good lately."

Recalling my thoughts on the moralizing of food choices, I immediately began to rewrite the dialogue in my head.

> "I'm in the mood for spinach dip. I realize I don't need
> your permission to order some, but I'm wondering if
> you'd care to share it with me."

"Sure! I'd love to. I'm aware that food choices really aren't 'good' or 'bad' and that too often, intake is confused with morality. In addition, I'm in the mood for the dip not because I've been restricting and now feel deserving and not because I've been restricting and now feel rebellious but because I'm simply in the mood for spinach dip."

That's much better.

Not long after, on a Manhattan sidewalk, I heard a conversation between a little girl, maybe 6 years old, and her father.

"Daddy, I'm hungry."

"Well, that's a shame, since you had ample opportunity to eat earlier."

I mentally crafted a more constructive version of Dad's response.

I'm sorry I couldn't design an eating schedule that matches your internal signals. I recognize, though, that hunger (especially at your age, when emotional eating hasn't had much time to develop) is largely a biological process and that, often, your hunger will not coincide with the meals we provide. It's important, though, to continue to honor your hunger (lest you develop eating problems later on), and for this reason, I think we should get you something to eat. Looking ahead, I'll make a note to always bring snacks along so that you don't feel so hungry again. In the future, I promise to validate your experiences (both physiological and emotional) and to avoid use of such erudite phrases as 'ample opportunity' until you're nine or ten.

EXERCISE: Rewriting the Conversation

For one week, keep a log/journal of all of the conversations that you hear about food and weight. How many did you hear? Where did you hear them? How did women portray their relationship with food or their bodies? How did you feel as you listened? I encourage you to choose a conversation that really bugged you and rewrite it—then submit it to me at my Eat in Peace website (http://eat-in-peace.com/contact). I'll pick the best examples to share with everyone on my blog.

Conclusion

The everyday language we hear and use creates powerful messages about the nature of our bodies and how they are supposed to look. To fully shield yourself from these messages, you'd have to cut yourself off from everything and everyone you know. As one of my blog readers pointed out, "Images of thinness and what that means have been medicalized and demonized across so many cultural and institutional realms that it makes it hard to know where to start. It is very hard to recover from an eating disorder in this culture, not [in the] least because weight obsession is everywhere and you almost become abnormal for not constantly watching your weight."

It's not surprising that so many women are plagued by body shame and insecurity. We've received these messages, in various forms and from various sources, from the time we were little girls. Combating the force of the messages requires attention to and modification of our own language, vigilance around even subtle communications from friends, family, advertising, and the media, and a commitment to deconstructing and disempowering the words we use.

Freeing yourself from exposure to toxic language is hard, but not impossible. You can start by taking a lead from Jessica Weiner, who suggests we respond to conversations spoken in the "Language of Fat" with, "Sorry, I don't speak that language."[29]

In the next chapter, I'll be looking at celebrities—a group of women whose bodies are constantly a topic of conversation, both positive and negative, and how this scrutiny is bad not just for them, but for all of us.

CHAPTER 4

⁄⁄⁄ The Role of Celebrity Worship

You can never be too rich or too thin.
— WALLIS SIMPSON

ARE BRITNEY SPEARS AND JESSICA SIMPSON TOO FAT? Does Kate Bosworth have an eating disorder? What kind of squats does Jessica Alba practice to tone her thighs? If search-engine visits to my blog are any indication, we can't get enough of celebrity bodies—admiring them, analyzing them, imitating them, and disparaging them. Throughout the course of writing this book, I became especially attuned to the attention afforded to celebrities' weight and shape. During my early blogging days, in one week alone, three of the most widely circulated celebrity weeklies hit the newsstands with their covers beckoning variations on a single theme:

- "Body Confessions," *In Touch*, July 24, 2006

- "Extreme Diets: Inside Hollywood's Dangerous Obsession with Being Thin," *US Weekly*, July 24, 2006

- "The New Lipo: New Procedure Melts Fat & Tightens Skin in Minutes!—& It's Affordable!," *Star*, July 24, 2006

In a *New York Times Magazine* article focusing on the dearth of leading roles for women in Hollywood, Lynn Hirschberg notes, "One place actresses are still the dominant forces is on the newsstand. Female stars may not sell tickets, but they do sell magazines."[1] If there's anything that piques our curiosity about celebrities (aside from their romances and children), it's their bodies. Coverage of celebrity figures and physiques seems to be proliferating at lightning speed across all media: magazines, talk shows and television tabloids, and Internet sites. One popular and active site, The Skinny Website, features celebrity body gossip and uses star photos to highlight celebrities' noticeable weight losses or gains. At one time the site offered page categories including "Skinny Celebrities," "Super Skinny," and "Scary Skinny."

It's hard enough to be a regular woman with a body image problem; imagine having your bikini body plastered across the covers of tabloids. It seems that we can now barely pick up a magazine without reading a feature about famous women's bodies—their diets, their product endorsements, their "pregnancy" watches, and their personal body image struggles. In this chapter, I discuss the collective impact of this focus and how it contributes to our growing problem of eating disordered thoughts, feelings, and behaviors, particularly among young women, who often worship the ever-shrinking celebrity as the beauty ideal.

Celebrity Diets

The morsel diet, invented by Mariah Carey, allows you to eat whatever you want, "but it has to be less than a forkful." This is just one example of a celebrity diet I found.[3] You've probably seen something similar in your reading; you don't have to search hard to find the latest celebrity craze. Low-

---

THIN SELLS—BUT DOES IT HAVE TO?

A 2012 study showed that when women were exposed to images of larger women, they tended to become more tolerant of larger frames and less preferential toward thinner bodies. Researchers noted that the women's "thinness preferences at posttest were significantly lower than at pretest." What might this mean? A shift toward normal-size (read: not ultra-thin) actors and models could create a greater tolerance and appreciation for a variety of body types.[2]

carb, high-protein, low-salt, minimeals—stars endorse various plans, helping these diets achieve a larger audience. After all, if it worked for her, it might work for the rest of us. Who wouldn't want the secret to high-fashion, red-carpet form? Celebrity diets provide even more fodder for a nation fixated on weight loss, even if (and often, especially if) the measures are unhealthy and extreme.

The problem, of course, is that eating less than a forkful of anything is a restrictive, compulsive way of enjoying one's food. Diet tips or secrets like this can seem innocent enough, but they encourage disordered eating—especially among young girls and adolescents reading fashion magazines. One offhand celebrity diet tip can be the start of a slow, insidious process culminating in disordered eating. In my practice, I've heard many eating disorder stories begin with some variation of, "I went on my first diet at 9 years old."

Madeline, a 21-year-old college senior, is one example. She remembers vividly the time her mother let her stay up to watch the Academy Awards with her when she was just a little girl. When actress Gwyneth Paltrow took the stage to accept her Best Actress award, Madeline was transfixed. "I was just seven," she said. "But I remember thinking she looked like such a princess, skinny and blonde and in that pretty pink dress."

As she entered her teenage years, Madeline continued to admire Paltrow and began to study how she ate—the macrobiotic diet, the detoxes, and elimination. Madeline dabbled in each for a bit and then gave up, finding Paltrow's plans too difficult to maintain. But then something shifted when she moved away from home. Now a theater major and aspiring actress, Madeline shifted her motivation to lose weight into overdrive. She scoured Paltrow's website and purchased her books, juiced in the morning and ate a restrictive diet the rest of the day, taking Paltrow's methods to the extreme. Madeline took delight in her weight loss, and her goal weight became a moving target. She reasoned that the skinnier she was, the more roles she might get and the more successful she'd be—just like Gwyneth.

What most readers forget is that celebrity advice is often unrealistic. Unlike commoners, celebrities have the luxury of personal trainers, chefs, and hours spent at the gym. Their bodies set a standard most of us cannot achieve without the same advantages. Supermodel Adriana Lima is a perfect example. In a 2011 interview with the *Telegraph*, we learn of all the work that goes into making Lima's body runway ready for a Victoria's Secret lingerie show:

> She sees a nutritionist, who has measured her body's muscle mass, fat ratio and levels of water retention. He prescribes protein shakes, vitamins and supplements to keep Lima's energy levels up during this training period. Lima drinks a gallon of water a day. For nine days before the show, she will drink only protein shakes—"no solids." The concoctions include powdered egg. Two days before the show, she will abstain from the daily gallon of water, and "just drink normally." Then, 12 hours before the show, she will stop drinking entirely. "No liquids at all so you dry out, sometimes you can lose up to eight pounds just from that," she says.[4]

To mold her body, Lima also puts herself through a grueling, full-time exercise regimen akin to Olympic training. Most of us can't take the time and don't have the money to do the same (nor do we have Lima's model looks, height, or frame). Still, she and other stars we love set the standard for us. The more we see of them, the more difficult it is to accept ourselves with all of our relative imperfections.

Too Fat/Too Thin

While researching this book, I spotted a cover story in the April 2, 2007, issue of *Life & Style* magazine "Skinny 911: Crazy diets! Extreme Workouts! Why Hollywood's Biggest Stars Are So Obsessed with Their Shrinking Bodies." An adjacent feature appearing as a side note said, "Look who's doing better!" and reported on other too-thin stars who'd put on a few pounds. Despite their healthy weight gains, all three of these recovering actresses were still underweight. All three may at some point be subjected to the health consequences of their too-thin histories. All three, in spite of their healthful trend, continued to model an unrealistic ideal for American women.

The media (or as I call them, "the weight patrol") love to watch celebrities like a hawk, establishing a virtual tipping point between "too fat" and "too thin." If a celebrity is too fat ("fat," here, being an incredibly relative term),

ALARMING BODY TRENDS

Remember "Madonna arms?" In recent years, a number of body trends have crept up in the national media: concave stomachs, bony backs, protruding hipbones, thigh gaps. Can you think of any others? How do these trends start? Why are they dangerous to model?

she'll be lambasted, ordered to cover up, or accused of being pregnant. If she's too thin, eating disorder rumors arise. The stars are caught in the middle and the public is left confused. Is drastic weight loss healthy (or even possible)? How thin is too thin? What is a normal weight? To shake the wrong kind of media attention and to secure the right kind (praise, support), stars end up dieting to quiet their critics. For example, a few years ago, questions arose in the media about whether the TV show *American Idol* had a body bias. Following full-figured Mandisa Hundley's performance, judge Simon Cowell infamously commented, "Do we have a bigger stage this year?" Fashion director of *InStyle* magazine Hal Rubenstein summed up the music industry's thin bias (and Cowell's): "Whether it's acting or anywhere, people do tend to want to look at pretty people first.... It is about packaging, especially nowadays. Does Britney have a great voice? Does Jessica? Who cares? Look what they look like. And it's an unfair world: I think it's more so for women than for men."[5]

Indeed, public interest in female performers' pop careers seems to peak only after they've lost weight—and then there's a greater interest in how they dropped the pounds (e.g., Jennifer Hudson) than in their voices or concert dates. Mandisa paid attention to this lesson. When I appeared with her on a *Today Show* panel on body image, she had lost a significant amount of weight. It's no coincidence that she was promoting her new album at the time.

Handlers, the media, and the public tell female celebrities, "Lose weight and boost your audience appeal." But what happens when they lose too much weight? Every once in a while, a star crosses the line and wanders into territory that, even with our unrealistic standards of weight and shape, we know to be too thin. Media attention increases, and a flurry of concern ensues, speculating about a potential eating disorder. Journalists ask, "Does she or doesn't she?"—losing sight of the fact that this is only speculation and that only a trained mental health professional can diagnose a disorder.

When I first started researching this topic, Nicole Richie was photographed wearing a light blue bikini and jogging on the beach. The media ate this image up, accusing Richie of having an eating disorder and dropping too much weight. Yet just a few years before, a reporter had asked Richie if she thought her "thickness" may prevent her from "getting certain parts."[6] More recently, tabloids accused Jennifer Hudson of going from too fat to too thin, taking her Weight Watchers endorsement to the extreme. And Miley Cyrus, having dropped her baby fat, is now referred to as wasting away. Can a celebrity ever get it right?

Media coverage of suspected or confirmed eating disorders is rampant, but it rarely affords the serious tone and attention these disorders deserve. The Hollywood Gossip (http://www.thehollywoodgossip.com), for example, once showcased an entire category of posts on eating disorders. One reader poll posed the question, "Which emaciated star will disappear first?"[7] Journalism of this nature continues to misrepresent the facts and undermine the gravity of eating disorders. As we witness celebrities becoming thinner and thinner, I've noticed a greater trend toward misinformation, armchair diagnoses, and jokes about eating disorders.

Kelly Clarkson is one example of a celebrity who's been the subject of such jokes. An online celebrity site posted an article about her six-month battle with bulimia in high school, accompanied by a current photo of her at the beach.[8] Hundreds of comments poured in. I had the chance to scroll through some of them. I forget sometimes, writing a body-friendly blog, just how angry and hateful the public can be:

> "From the looks of that picture, she should think about starting up [her bulimia] again."

> "I think this pic was snapped just as she started to hurl. Way to go Kelly! There is a thin you trapped somewhere in there."

Fortunately, Kelly had some defenders:

"She is NOT FAT at all. I don't see cellulite, rolls or a belly. She's just not super skinny. Part of the reason people become bulimic is because of comments like this."

"I'd love to see how you measure up against an incredibly normal-looking human being having fun at the beach.... so many of the commenters have really f------up views of what is good/beautiful/acceptable/normal. You're all so brainwashed to think that women who are so Hollywood thin are normal."

The inaccurate, hurtful, angry, violent, and misogynistic comments on this post set up an impossible body image ideal, encouraged eating disorders as worthy or effective tools for weight loss, and put forth misconceptions about bulimia (e.g., that only very thin women suffer from it). They also attacked a star in recovery from an eating disorder by denying her right to self-acceptance. So much for honesty. It's a dangerous world out there, one where a star's alleged appeal (or lack thereof) is up for public—often cruel—debate.

Contradicting the too-fat comments about Kelly is a *Details* magazine feature entitled "Why Fat Is Back in Hollywood," in which writer Holly Millea discusses how the superthin look is slowly being countered by a curvy, more feminine look, reminiscent of old Hollywood and pinup stars. (Think Katy Perry or Scarlett Johansson.) I'm always interested in journalism that confronts body stereotypes. At first, Millea's premise seems positive. The article's subtitle says, "In an industry rife with painfully thin stick figures, women with some meat on their bones are—lucky for us—rising to the top." But despite her intention to expand the definition of feminine beauty, Millea inadvertently objectifies celebrities further (while laying on a heavy dose of snarkiness):

You see that look in the faces of formerly fleshy sexpots who have morphed into pinched, prematurely aged superwaifs. What do they do for fun? Food and sex are appetites inextricably linked in the human psyche. One could speculate that for those obsessed with not eating, even the boyfriend's salami goes the way of the bread basket.[9]

Millea's message is a classic weight patrol cry: "Too thin!" Instead of expressing concern for the "superwaifs," she implies that they can't be sex objects anymore. Don't starve yourself skinny—not because it isn't healthy or because it irreparably damages your psyche and your will to live, or even because it sets up an often deadly, unrealistic standard for your fans, but because *too skinny* is not so sexy. Hit them where it hurts and maybe we'll gain some ground.

In the same article, Millea realizes the challenge we face in trying to accept "lush," "curvy" forms, particularly in Hollywood:

> Of course, it's easy for anyone who isn't an aspiring actress to beat the drum for weight gain. Our careers don't depend on being a jean size smaller than the next girl. As one male studio executive who asked not to be named says, "Do we really want stars to look like the rest of us? If actresses represented the way the public really looks, the mother from *Gilbert Grape* would be a sex symbol."[10]

In other words, let's not get carried away. Old-school pinup figures are okay, but if we're too accepting of celebrity curves, if we accept greater than zero as body-beautiful, then we're just a couple of steps away from accepting morbid obesity in others and ourselves. Like the diet and fashion industries, entertainment has billions invested in this belief. Diminishing bodies are products. They sell fashion endorsements, book contracts, and free publicity. If a star gains weight, we pay attention. If she loses weight, we may pay even more attention. As consumers of celebrity culture, we're not completely blameless. We chant from the sidelines, "Thinner, thinner, thinner, thinner!" until, "Oops—too thin." Skinny is desirable, but when someone develops anorexia, that's where we draw the line.

Pregnancy Rumors

I'm pregnant. So, apparently, are all of you.

It seems that celebrity gossip columnists are perennially on the lookout for stars with a bump—any abdomen that is not concave in form. File this under reasons to be grateful you're not a celebrity. True, bump sightings sometimes result in real-life embryos, but in their zeal to predict celebrity

CELEBRITIES SPEAK OUT

"You're damned if you're too thin and you're damned if you're too heavy. According to the press I've been both. It's impossible to satisfy everyone and I suggest we stop trying."—Jennifer Aniston

"I remember everyone asking when I was doing press for the movie 'What did you do to look so thin? You looked great' and I'm like, 'I looked emaciated'…It's a form of violence, in the way that we look at women and how we expect them to look and be—for what sake? Not health, not survival, not enjoyment of life but just so you could look pretty. I'm constantly telling girls all the time, 'Everything's airbrushed, everything's retouched. None of us look like that."—Rosario Dawson

"Anytime someone talks about your figure constantly, you get nervous, you get really self-conscious. I was working my butt off on the show, and then all anyone was talking about was my body."—Christina Hendricks of *Mad Men*[11]

reproduction, reporters often jump the gun, creating a baby out of a hearty meal, a form-fitting dress, or, heaven forbid, some additional weight. A few years back, Sandra Bullock responded to an *Extra* reporter's query about a possible pregnancy: "It's called weight gain."[12] I just loved her get-over-it response.

But Bullock's not the only star with a false positive pregnancy. Other celebrities also touted incorrectly as with child include Jennifer Aniston, Jennifer Lopez, Khloé Kardashian, Mila Kunis, and Lady Gaga. Jennifer Aniston seems to be labeled pregnant each time she wears a flowing top, carries an oversized bag, or puts on a couple of pounds. In fact, if Aniston had had a baby each time a gossip mag accused her of being pregnant, she'd be rivaling the Duggars for family size!

If a pregnancy is in fact confirmed, we continue to watch and judge. Stars are criticized for gaining too much pregnancy weight (e.g., Kim Kardashian, Jessica Simpson, Salma Hayek), not enough (the Duchess of Cambridge, Victoria Beckham), or of faking the entire pregnancy (Beyoncé, Katie Holmes,

Nicole Kidman, Kelly Preston). It seems impossible to get it right. Even Angelina Jolie has been subject to speculations about her pregnancy weight. Apparently, the months required to lose baby weight in a natural and healthy way are far too slow for the average news cycle. As one of my blog readers noted around the time of one of Jolie's deliveries, "The world is waiting right now to see how much weight Angelina has lost in the five days since she had her baby. No wonder she is hiding in Africa....I wouldn't want the world judging me either."

Though it's apparently acceptable to stalk celebrity abdomens from afar, in real life, social graces encourage us to avoid the pregnancy question like the plague. Nothing could be worse than identifying a false positive. I think we'll know our culture has settled into a healthy place regarding weight and shape when we're able to ask the pregnancy question ("Are you?") as easily as any other ("Did you cut your hair?" "Did you get some sun?") because the potential connotation of weight gain won't be the dagger it is today.

By the way, congratulations to all of us—I'm having, as you can probably guess from the size of my bump, twins.

Stars Who Struggle

You may know, or have suspected, that being surrounded by images of thin, toned celebrities like Jennifer Aniston can make you more aware of your own flaws. One study conducted at Ryerson University in 2009 proved it. Researchers learned that watching a ten-minute clip from the TV show *Friends* (starring Aniston, Courteney Cox, and Lisa Kudrow—all thin actresses) was associated with adverse effects on female viewers' own body image. (The good news: study participants who were primed before the clip with material highlighting how unrealistic and unattainable television images of women can be had a less negative outcome on body satisfaction.)[13]

Stars themselves, however, also struggle with the perfect body ideal. Our scrutiny of celebrity bodies frequently can contribute to disordered behavior and full-blown eating disorders. You may recall an episode in season 3 of *Sex and the City,* in which Charlotte York (Kristin Davis) conquers the health-club steam room, quelling her weight and shape fears by finally baring it all. Throughout the episode, Charlotte struggles with body image concerns, frequently comparing herself to others. She resolves her body conflict only after another woman in the steam room compliments her on her breasts. (Approval from a woman with a body she admires being the only way she can feel good about herself.)[14]

Actress Kristin Davis later revealed to Scotland's *Daily Record* that, like Charlotte, she struggled with eating and body image concerns. "Everyone [in the cast] would talk about their diets and working out, and what it made me do was go to craft services—where all the food for the cast and crew was—and I would eat." As compensation for this eating, Ms. Davis began to run seven miles at a pop. In regard to her overexercising, she noted, "I was killing myself. My ankles hurt, my knees hurt and I was working 18-hour days."[15]

Media attention may have contributed to her predicament. When Ms. Davis first joined the show's cast, a reporter noted she'd be too heavy for the lead role, based on the life of ultrathin Candace Bushnell. The role ultimately went to Sarah Jessica Parker, and damages were awarded to Davis, who revealed that following the reporter's comment, "I tried not to cry and said I had to leave," after which, she binged on cookies, thinking, "To hell with you, I'm going to eat what I want."[16]

Other stars, like Paula Abdul, Portia de Rossi, Lady Gaga, Mary-Kate Olsen, Katie Couric, Alanis Morissette, Calista Flockhart, and Jamie-Lynn Sigler have all been open about their eating disordered pasts; the latter is now a National Eating Disorders Association ambassador.

A while back, a reporter asked me my position regarding celebrities disclosing that they have struggled with eating disorders. She asked if I thought the disclosure was helpful or hurtful for the general public. While I'm never happy to hear that a star has developed a full-fledged eating disorder, I believe it's helpful for the public to know that unnatural thinness among

SNEAKY BIASES

You know those "Who Wore It Better?" features in magazines? On what basis do you judge the winner? Is this competition more about fashion or physique? And, why are we making these women compete with each other over who looks better for the purposes of our entertainment?

celebrity women is, in fact, unnatural. In many cases, celebrities and models (like Adriana Lima) must go to drastic measures to conform to our current body ideal. For some, these measures may contribute to the development of full-blown eating disorders. In my opinion, the more information we have that counteracts the idea that skinny is healthy and effortless for all women, the better. I also feel that for fans who struggle with eating disorders, learning of someone else's struggle may help with feelings of shame or isolation.

EXERCISE: Celebrity Appeal

Often, our consumption of celebrity media makes us feel bad about ourselves. Try out these tips for addressing this concern:

1. Limit your exposure to media that promotes an unrealistic ideal. If fashion magazines cause you to feel bad about your body, go on a fashion magazine diet.

2. Remind yourself of the electronic manipulation of photos that magazines use to make stars appear more attractive.

3. Consume media that presents more realistic images of women. In *Glamour* magazine's September 2009 issue, a photo of plus-size model Lizzie Miller created a media sensation. Miller was captured in print, leaning over in a pose that caused her stomach to buckle—as would many women's! Can you find other images of more realistic bodies?

4. Locate celebrity role models who seem to have positive relationships with food and their bodies. Besides the women quoted earlier, who else can you think of?

5. Remember that comparing your body to a celebrity's is a losing proposition. Stars are paid for their appearance and often have unattainable looks. Instead, make a commitment to appreciating yourself and your unique constellation of features and flesh without a comparison to the thinner or shapelier images that beckon you from the movies, television, and magazines.

Conclusion

Amid all the media messages that fuel body hatred, there are a few glimpses of late of celebrities, writers, and public figures who offer body-positive statements and examples. Current film sensation Jennifer Lawrence, for example, recently told *Life & Style* magazine that she, for one, is not going hungry. "I remember when I was 13 and it was cool to pretend to have an eating disorder because there were rumors that Lindsay Lohan and Nicole Richie were anorexic." Now considered somewhat plump for Hollywood, Lawrence feels differently. "I'm just so sick of these young girls with diets. I think it's really important for girls to have people to look up to and feel good about themselves."[17]

I hope that we can look back in five or ten years and see that the tide has changed. When we continue to see celebrities deflate from one magazine issue to another, we begin to internalize even more improbable ideas about how our bodies should look. The reality is that only a very small percentage of people have "model looks," and yet the great majority of us are continuously working toward or berating ourselves for not achieving this ideal. Arriving at a healthier place with regard to food and weight will ultimately depend on our recognizing that our thoughts and preferences related to shape are a direct result of our viewing these matters through a culturally sanctioned, thinner-is-better lens. My hope is that someday we can reach a point where nobody's weight or shape, no matter how famous she is, is a topic of conversation. Before we can get there, however, we need to tackle our phobia of fat and what's behind it. By promoting thin, are we really promoting health? In chapter 5, I look closely at whether fat really is the problem we make it out to be.

CHAPTER 5

⁄⁄⁄ Fat Isn't the Problem

Every weight loss program,
no matter how positively it's packaged,
whispers to you that you're not right.
You're not good enough.
You're unacceptable and you need to be fixed.

—KIM BRITTINGHAM,
Read My Hips: How I Learned to Love My Body,
Ditch Dieting, and Live Large

MOST OF US ARE PROBABLY FAMILIAR with Albert Einstein's definition of insanity—doing the same thing over and over again and expecting different results. However, you wouldn't know it from our addiction to diet plans. Our $61 billion (and counting) diet industry is proof that women are, according to Einstein's definition, insane—or at least practicing an insane behavior by trying diet after diet, somehow hoping that *this one* will be the one that works—and lasts.[1]

A variety of cultural influences have convinced us that if we're not watching our weight and fighting the battle of the bulge, we're doing something wrong. Yet is carrying a little extra fat really such a big deal? You're probably aware of the health consequences associated with being overweight. News stories, daytime TV doctors, weight-loss reality shows, women's magazines, and even your own physician encourage you to maintain a healthy weight at all costs. But what is a healthy weight, and how is it defined (and by whom)? Are fat and the "obesity epidemic" really the problems we're meant to believe they are?

In this chapter, I'll address these questions while looking critically at the diet industry, obesity research, and our reliance on BMI as a measure of health. You may be surprised to learn that the relationship between weight and health isn't as clear as you think.

Diets Don't Work

"When I was 16 years old, I traveled to the States (from Germany) with my family, and we stayed with an American family in Virginia." So began a note from one of my blog readers. "Mother, father, and daughter all were overweight. Both mother and daughter ate only low-fat fare. Low-fat mayonnaise, low-fat milk, low-fat cream cheese...you name it. They couldn't believe my mom was feeding her entire family full-fat milk, butter, and cheeses. To them, that almost seemed like a crime. And yet—our entire family was lean and healthy. Hmmm."

Frustrating, isn't it? We Americans work so hard to watch our weight while foreigners eat what they like and manage to stay more slender. (Thus the popularity of the 2007 diet book *French Women Don't Get Fat*.) Perhaps Europeans, with their more satisfying meals, recognize something we don't—diets don't work. If you begin a diet, yes, chances are you'll lose weight. But chances are you'll gain the weight back when you stop dieting. One recent study in the *Journal of Adolescent Health* noted, "Findings clearly indicate that dieting and unhealthy weight-control behaviors, as reported by adolescents, predict significant weight gain over time."[2] Research out of UCLA in 2007 looked at a number of weight-loss studies and concluded that "Dieting leads to more weight gain over time than not dieting." Regarding the obese population for which dieting is most often recommended, the researchers went on to say that "the benefits of dieting are simply too small and the potential harms of dieting are too large for it to be recommended as a safe and effective treatment for obesity."[3]

After you stop dieting, you will likely gain back the pounds, and often even surpass your starting weight. Along with those extra rebound pounds comes another unfortunate side effect—the feeling of failure.

We know that diets fail—but why? As I discussed in chapter 2, the diet-binge cycle is partly to blame. When you cut back on calories or restrict certain foods, you can end up triggering overeating as a result. But even those who don't end up bingeing still manage to regain. Neuroscientist and author Dr. Sandra Aamodt, who gave a powerful TED Talk in 2013, says our brains are evolutionarily hardwired to maintain our weight, explaining why dieting efforts typically backfire. Just like a thermostat, the brain controls weight through a feedback loop that impacts hunger and metabolism. If we lose weight on a diet, powerful forces kick in to combat this perceived starvation—our metabolism slows and our hunger increases. Aamodt explained that it isn't a lack of willpower that causes diets to fail but a brain committed to a particular set point of weight.[4]

One of my blog readers, Lara, has firsthand experience with this phenomenon. An active and outdoorsy person, Lara for years had avoided partaking in the eating disordered behavior of her peers (including her best friend from high school, who struggled first with anorexia and then bulimia). When she took her first real job after college, however, the sedentary lifestyle led her to gain some weight. She decided to make some changes:

> I made a conscious decision to start eating healthier and got a gym membership. The token "5 lbs" that I had wanted to lose came off, and I continued on my new routine. My weight dropped lower. I've always been athletic, and at 5'3" am probably healthiest at my average weight of 120. A few pounds may not mean much, but working out daily and restricting calories caused a loss that dropped me into a less practical range. I thought this weight loss was akin to health, but my constant hunger and increasing unwillingness to take a day off from the gym lest I feel guilty, told me otherwise.
>
> I didn't listen to these signals, and one day I found myself devouring whatever I could find in the apartment. Food was always on my mind; I wasn't even finished chewing my first meal of the day before already plotting

and yearning for my second. My "splurge" takeout meal on Sunday nights would get me through the week, and once I got there, I'd eat so much, preparing for the hibernation of the week to come, that it caused the most uncomfortable feeling.

Overall, I was confused by these binges. I was eating so healthily. Why did I have to do this? I started eating bigger meals at night and eased up on the restriction, but the bingeing continued sporadically. I still remember the day that I decided I hated being so uncomfortably full and decided to purge. I was angry and baffled at myself, and all I could think of was my friend from high school. I was in my mid-twenties—why was this happening to me now? I saw girls go through it, and I know the havoc it can wreak on your body and emotions, but here I was, voluntarily putting myself in the same position...I never wanted to be stick thin, and I believe when I look in the mirror I do see the real me, but I still chose to lose a few pounds.

EXERCISE: Your Diet History

Have you ever dieted and gained back the weight? How much weight did you gain back after each diet? Try making a time line plotting your dieting efforts and your weight over the years. What do you notice? Did you gain weight after each diet attempt? If so, maybe dieting isn't working for you.

The obvious solution to "diets fail" seems to be the mantra "Try harder"; yet Lara's efforts were noble and she still ended up bingeing. It turns out, researchers have found, that as Dr. Aamodt suggests willpower goes only so far. You may have less control over your weight, shape, and size than you think. In her book *Rethinking Thin: The New Science of Weight Loss—and the Myths and Realities of Dieting*, health journalist Gina Kolata set out on a quest to find out the truth about dieting and whether it works. Setting the backdrop for her book is a study headquartered at the University of Pennsylvania, comparing the effects of two popular diets—low-fat, low-calorie (conventional diet) versus low-carb (Atkins)—on weight and health. Participants in the Atkins group lost more weight the first six months of the diet than those in the conventional diet group, but both groups showed rather unimpressive weight-loss numbers. A significant portion of dieters dropped out of the study, and after a year's time, almost everyone in both groups who had lost weight had regained the bulk of it. Those in the Atkins group showed greater weight regain after one year, suggesting that losing more weight was associated with gaining more weight back.[5]

After reviewing these findings and many others from the fields of weight science and genetics, Kolata concluded that "no matter what the diet and no matter how hard they try, most people will not be able to lose a lot of weight and keep it off."[6] Your body's hunger and satiety hormones and chemicals such as ghrelin, neuropeptide Y, and leptin all regulate appetite beyond your conscious control. With genetics, hormones, brain circuitry, and early nutrition all factors, diet is only one small piece of the puzzle. In the end, she says, we really don't have much control over what we weigh.

A 2005 study by University of California, Davis, researchers seems to support this theory. The researchers compared two groups of obese, chronic dieters for a period of two years. One group followed a standard diet and exercise protocol; the other practiced a "Health at Every Size" approach (intuitive eating—eating according to hunger and fullness cues—and participating in enjoyable physical activity). After six months, both groups demonstrated health and psychological improvements, but only the dieters had dropped pounds. The diet worked—at first.

At the two-year follow-up, however, the diet group had regained most of the weight they'd lost. They'd also lost the health improvements they'd previously achieved and reported reduced self-esteem. Dieting actually seemed to do them harm. By comparison, the "Health at Every Size" participants, whose focus was on wellness rather than weight loss, had remained at their prestudy weight and showed increased self-esteem, decreased depression, a decrease in some eating disordered behaviors, and improved physical functioning (sustained lower cholesterol and blood pressure levels over time).[7]

The harder you try to control your weight, the less control you seem to have. Perhaps fat people are not to blame for their size; reducing, for many of us, is a never-ending battle against our genes.

If this is true, then why do we persist in dieting? As Kolata writes, "Who could miss the drumbeat of messages from scientists and weight-loss experts, the incessant hectoring year in and year out, assuring fat people that everything is possible for those who really, really try?"[8] Even she, the objective science journalist with all the facts at hand, found herself drawn in by the diet allure, cheerleading four of the obese dieters whose progress she tracked for her book: "I wanted it so much that I began to suspend disbelief. I knew, I knew, the science and the overwhelmingly convincing evidence that most obese people will not be able to diet, get thin, and stay at a new low weight. But…I allowed myself to think that maybe, just maybe these people would make it. Maybe they would fulfill their dreams."[9]

. . . .

ASSIGNMENT: A New Mantra

"Dieting is all about willpower." This belief isn't helping you. I propose a new mantra to replace it: "Have the willpower not to diet!" Most people blame themselves when they can't keep to a diet or when they gain back the weight following a dieting attempt. But given the research, can you really blame yourself? Start blaming diets for being unrealistic and offering false promises without any long-term hope. End this unhealthy relationship for good.

. . . .

How the Diet Industry Profits

Data doubting the efficacy of diets have spoken loud and clear, and not one product, plan, or gimmick has shown the ability to compete successfully with the facts. Yet every day, obesity researchers and scientists continue to run studies, forever searching for the weight-loss holy grail. Why? Because an entire $60 billion industry rests on the possibility of autonomic weight control. If you can be convinced that your shape and size are completely your responsibility and that you have the power to mold yourself into something new, you'll keep trying, spending hundreds or thousands of dollars to get the results you want.

When one popular diet proves unsuccessful in helping you get and stay thin, another one always rises up to take its place. When I was in college, fat was the enemy. Low fat, reduced fat, no fat, fat free—whatever you did, you just had to stay clear of fat. And therefore, legions of coeds feasted on the Final Four: salad, cereal, bagels, and fat-free frozen yogurt. Mix and match, and you'd be fed for weeks. During this time, I discovered fat-free brownies (suggested motto: "One—not so good; half a batch—*remotely* satisfying") and similar products high in sugar, multisyllabic chemicals, and other fillers all designed to not-so-successfully compensate for the glaring absence of fat.

But fat-free diets don't always make for fat-free people. Someone finally noticed that 5,000 calories a day of fat-free cereal could indeed make you fat. In response, we struck a peace deal and waged war against carbohydrates instead. Low carb, no carb, Atkins, South Beach, the Zone Diet—fat was now an ally! In this new climate, you were invited to chew your gravy, as long as it was carb-free. Again, instead of eating natural, whole foods, we turned to artificial options like low-carb bagels (how does that work?), sugar-free chocolate, and Tasti D-Lite.

When we realized that too much animal fat wasn't good for our health, we backed off on ribs and chicken wings, but we're still a low-carb, high-chemical nation today. (Try picking out a sports drink at your gym's refrigerated case. It's tough to find a healthy option. Sugar-free—maybe. Natural? No. Many are infused with artificial sweeteners.)

Almost every fad diet and eating plan spawns products, including books, subscription websites, and branded food items you can either buy at the store or have delivered to your home. How much money are they making?

Diet Plan	Estimated Revenue
The Atkins Diet	$66,700,000
The South Beach Diet	$1 to 2.5 million
The Zone Diet	$2,400,000
Jenny Craig	$343,000,000
Nutrisystem	$396,900,000[10]

What's important to keep in mind is that these diets don't have a long-lasting effect—which means that if you want to get and stay slim, you must stay on them forever. The diet industry thrives because each plan deprives you of something your body wants, whether it be fat, carbs, or sufficient calories. When you stop a diet and begin to reintroduce nutrients in the form of forbidden foods (e.g., potatoes, cheese, a hamburger), your cravings remit—your body's way of saying, "Thanks for giving me what I need." When the weight comes back, you panic and start on another diet.

Because in today's world carbs are the enemy, you may be avoiding bread and starchy vegetables. Yes, you may weigh a little less as a result, but what you don't realize is that you're eliminating a major energy source, one that fuels your muscles, organs, and brain. Carbohydrates have a significant impact on mood, as well. Just ask someone who's going totally carb-free—grumpiness and bouts of depression are not uncommon. Not one nutritionist I respect has ever recommended a low-carb diet to anyone I know because nutritionists understand the importance of all three macronutrients—protein, fat, and carbohydrates. Without them, you're setting yourself up to fail.

I use myself as a case study for the danger in adhering to a diet plan that deprives your body of what it needs. Years ago, as a busy vegetarian, I was looking for quick, nutritious meals that didn't break the bank. A coworker swore by the Zone Diet. The convenience of home delivery won me over, so I gave the vegetarian program a try, communicating to the sales representative that I wasn't interested in weight loss, just easy, balanced meals. Soon, my balanced meals were eight servings of tofu a day—for breakfast, lunch, dinner, and a snack before bed. As I write this, I stand firm in my belief that tofu is not a breakfast food, no matter how closely it resembles a sausage link.

During my Zone Diet trial, I got really, really hungry, which didn't make sense since I hadn't selected a weight-loss plan. Two days into the program, I went to the gym and quickly realized my efforts were at about 50 percent. I felt tired and weak and soon became so dizzy and faint that I barely made it home. My normal blood pressure is about 90/60, and I could tell I was dangerously south of that. I considered going to the closest ER, but first I planted myself at the computer and searched the panacea for all things medical—the web. I learned that such meal plans (particularly for the uninitiated) often create electrolyte imbalances and that salt ingestion was a quick and effective cure. I ate some crackers and slowly began to feel better and more myself.

After that experience, I tossed the remaining meals and ended my time in the Zone. A week later, I got a call from a program rep. "How did the diet go?"

I explained how hungry, tired, and sick I became. His response: "I'm sorry to hear that. We're offering a discount for the monthly program, which would be only $36.95 a day. Would you like to enroll?"

I didn't rebound or gain any extra weight when I dropped the Zone, but I was offered an opportunity to spend about $13,000 a year on meals that would not even meet my basic survival needs.

While researching this book, I decided to go undercover to review another popular diet—the antidiet diet, Weight Watchers (WW). Many of my patients have enrolled over the years; women are always asking my opinion of the program. If you're unfamiliar, here's how Weight Watchers works: Members don't count calories, but rather points. They can eat any foods they want, as long as they consume a certain number of milks and oils, unlimited fruits and (most) vegetables, a limited amount of grains and proteins at every meal, and "Three to four points a day for goodies." Every day they tally the point value of each item, seeking to stay within a set daily or weekly amount designed for weight loss.

As flexible as the plan may be, Weight Watchers is still, at its core, a weight-loss plan focused on restriction. Before issuing an official stance, however, I decided to attend a meeting.

Just before noon on a hot summer day in New York City, I entered the building and climbed the steps to the second floor. The first thing I saw? The scales. I completed a registration form, greeted the lady behind the counter, handed her my card, and stated that I was there to try out a meeting.

"How tall are you?" she asked.

"Five feet five inches."

"Okay. Now put down your bag, take off your shoes, and step on the scale."

"Oh, I really don't need to be weighed."

"You have to be weighed. You don't have to look, and I won't tell you, but you have to be weighed to register."

"Oh, you see, I don't want to register. I just want to try out a meeting."

"See me at the end if you're interested in joining."

Having won my first battle as an undercover eating disorder specialist, I took a seat and surveyed the room, which contained a preponderance of already-thin women. I wondered if they were Weight Watchers success stories or if they were just starting out—Manhattan's take on "overweight."

A woman whom I'll call Marilyn began the meeting with a discussion about lapses—when WW members fall off the wagon and eat in excess of their points. She mentioned the tendency to overeat once you've already lapsed, rationalizing, "I'll never be thin anyway." I noted that her analysis was consistent with a cognitive therapy approach, focusing on the thought distortion known as black-and-white thinking (further explored in chapter 2).

Marilyn asked members why a lapse occurs. People volunteered some answers: stress, illness, missing meetings, attending dinner parties or special events. As solutions to lapses, members reiterated their commitment to plan their meals, come to meetings, and use their extra points. Marilyn then asked the group about their "last-straw incidents," the final pushes that brought them to Weight Watchers—such as seeing themselves in an unflattering photo or getting a doctor's advice to lose weight. She then transitioned to other ways people might handle their emotions, rather than reaching for food. Members offered suggestions: exercising, reading, talking to a friend. Here, Marilyn focused on enhancing coping resources and self-soothing techniques. I was impressed. Later, she returned to the experience of emotions and validated members' emotional experiences by stating, "You can't take a feeling away from somebody."

Throughout the meeting, members shared their stories. Marilyn praised them and handed out stickers as positive reinforcement. One woman revealed that following a meeting last week, she "immediately went out" and "was bad." As I've written earlier, there's no such thing as "bad" unless you're hurting someone else. I found it frustrating to hear her moralize her food choices, but I could certainly understand the need to rebel, particularly following a public weigh-in with its (intended?) consequent shame.

During this discussion, the topic of lifetime membership came up, which entitles members to free WW meetings. To qualify, members must reach and maintain their goal weight. Marilyn pointed out that if there's a bona fide reason you're unable to attain this goal, "You can get a doctor's note and Weight Watchers will accept that." At one point, Marilyn noted, "Having a plan like this makes you feel happy."

Marilyn closed the meeting by offering, "Think where you don't want to be again and where you want to go."

I got up to leave the meeting, filing past the diaries, food planners, and boxes of Weight Watchers brand Pretzel Thins, Smoothies, and Mini Bars lining the shelves, most of which were available to members for an added fee. On my way out, I ran across an older woman who'd sat in front of me during the talk with a banana and a Diet Coke on her lap (her lunch, I suspected).

"How long have you been coming here?" I overheard someone ask her.

"Forty years," she said.

At this writing, the annual cost of a Weight Watchers membership, meetings included, is about $515 per year.[11] Multiply that times forty years and you get $20,600. My hope is that she was a lifetime member.

My official opinion is that Weight Watchers is not 100 percent bad—it seems to offer a bare bones approach to healthy eating, provides social support, incorporates a number of sound psychological principles, and is less restrictive than most diets I know. Still, it is a diet, and as such promotes a fixation on counting, planning, and restrictions, all of which are disordered behaviors. Weight Watchers members get stressed about eating out or going to social functions, really any situation where they're unable to calculate their points. Inevitably, participation in such a diet arouses rebellion. I'm not surprised when I hear how various members have yo-yoed. When they gain weight, they feel they did so because they veered from the program. Getting back on the program, of course, costs money. Weight Watchers can be a lifelong journey for many women, which may be why, in 2012, the company raked in a reported $1.8 billion.[12]

Overweight Doesn't Mean Unhealthy: Rethinking BMI

In 1998, millions of Americans became overweight—overnight. This did not happen because of a sudden shift in the earth's gravity or a collective bout of sleep eating. In fact, most of those who woke up fat probably didn't gain an ounce. So what happened? The National Institutes of Health (NIH) decided

MYTHS ABOUT CALORIE LABELING

Many restaurants now label the calorie contents of foods they sell—a practice that's become a law in some places and was slated to become federal law in 2014. Is this really good for your health? Unfortunately, calories tell only a small piece of the equation. Consumers may choose lower-calorie foods at the expense of ignoring other nutritional data, like protein, carbohydrates, fat, salt, and fiber content, along with important vitamins and minerals that contribute to the value of certain foods. A small bag of almonds is more caloric than a similar serving of jelly beans but the almonds are more nutritious. If the calories alone are posted, which would you choose? Would it be the healthier choice?

to lower the BMI cutoff associated with the overweight category. The BMI is a simple measure, based on height and weight, that's commonly used to determine if someone is overweight. Millions of people went to bed at healthy weights, with BMIs up to 27 in women and 28 in men. When they woke up the next morning, the new BMI cutoff for overweight for both sexes was 25—meaning all of those previously healthy people were fat. Even some celebrities were reclassified as overweight. In his book *The Diet Myth: Why America's Obsession with Weight Is Hazardous to Your Health*, a study of the weight-loss research enterprise and industry, author Paul Campos offers a few examples of "fat" celebrities, according to the current BMI definitions (over 25 = overweight, over 30 = obese). Coming in as overweight are Brad Pitt, Michael Jordan, and Mel Gibson. Obese celebrities include Russell Crowe, George Clooney, and slugger Sammy Sosa.[13]

When policymakers and public health officials talk about the obesity crisis in America, they're usually referring to this seemingly arbitrary BMI data. Considering the host of variables that need to be taken into account when determining the actual health consequences of weight, this measurement is overly simplistic. After all, a person could be very heavy but mostly muscle. Considering BMI alone, increasing your fitness could actually result in a higher BMI and a new designation of overweight or obese.

BMI is not only a blunt and arbitrary measure, it's also ineffective at predicting health outcomes. Studies show that having a low BMI isn't necessarily a protective factor against disease and death. In fact, being on the thinner side could actually be more dangerous to your health. *The Lancet* medical journal published meta-analytic research conducted at the Mayo Clinic based on the results of forty different studies, suggesting that those with BMIs that were too low had a greater mortality risk than those who had BMIs in the normal range. People considered overweight according to BMI actually had a higher rate of survival (including a lower cardiovascular mortality) than those in the normal BMI range, while those who were obese did not evidence any increased mortality.[14]

But being obese has other dangers, right? You've probably heard the term "metabolic syndrome" in news stories. The Mayo Clinic defines it as "a cluster of conditions—increased blood pressure, a high-blood sugar level, excess body fat around the waist, and abnormal cholesterol levels—that occur together, increasing your risk of heart disease, stroke, and diabetes."[15] The problem with metabolic syndrome is that it's not so easy to detect based on an analysis of body size. A 2008 study published in the *Archives of Internal Medicine* found that 23.5 percent of "normal-weight" adults exhibited cardiometabolic abnormalities and that 51.3 percent of overweight (and 31.7 percent of obese) adults evidenced metabolic health.[16]

To me, these implications are striking. What this means is that those who are overweight or obese according to BMI may be mislabeled as ill (and treated medically as such) while those who are within the "healthy" BMI range, but who actually have metabolic disease, might not be identified and treated until later in their disease progression. BMI could not only be a poor predictor of health—it could also actually be leading us down the wrong path, treating people who don't need treatment while overlooking those who do.

I have provided links in the appendix to several other research articles that could persuade you, but here is the evidence that I found the most remarkable: being heavy can actually help you live longer with disease. In a 2012 *New York Times* article, journalist Harriet Brown looked into "the obesity paradox"—the idea that fat, contrary to popular belief, may actually be a protective factor toward longevity. Brown noted in the article that diabetes patients who are normal weight (again, using BMI as the measure) are twice as likely to die as their obese and overweight counterparts. "In study after study," she says, "overweight and moderately obese patients with certain chronic diseases often live longer and fare better than normal-weight patients with the same ailments."[17]

With everything we hear daily about the dangers of being overweight, who would believe that extra pounds could be good for us? Surely she made some mistake. Nope. Brown cites the research of epidemiologist Katherine Flegal, who found that the biggest risks of death are associated with being at either end of the BMI spectrum—either underweight or severely obese. People in the overweight category (BMIs of 25 to 30) enjoyed the lowest mortality risks, while those qualifying as moderately obese (30 to 35) were at no more risk for death than those in the normal-weight category.[18] In 2013, Flegal researched the topic further in an article in the *Journal of the American Medical Association*. She and her colleagues analyzed the results of ninety-seven different studies, and concluded that low-level obesity did not increase the risk of mortality and that being overweight was actually associated with decreased mortality.[19]

Other research I've seen suggests that being overweight cannot be definitively linked to common forms of heart disease, type 2 diabetes can go into remission without the need to drop weight (a nutritious diet and exercise are enough), and a little extra fat might have a positive or preventative effect on common types of cancer—including lung cancer and breast cancer—as well as osteoporosis and certain respiratory diseases.[20]

What can we draw from this knowledge? Assuming you're moving your body and eating mostly healthful foods, which I'd encourage everyone to do regardless of weight, a few extra pounds could actually add years to your life (and, probably, life to your years as you end the struggle to lose weight). We can also conclude that BMI is a minimally useful tool for predicting disease (though apparently very useful for separating "ideal" bodies from "nonideal," regardless of actual health or longevity concerns).

The truth is, there's really no way to evaluate anyone's health based on how she looks. There are plenty of fat, healthy people walking around. They're healthy because they eat nutritious foods and lead active lifestyles.

Similarly, there are plenty of thin, unhealthy people (you probably know a few) who eat a nonnutritious diet and are sedentary. What worries me is how often doctors, armed with BMI results, suggest that perfectly healthy, heavy women lose weight for the sake of their health. At the same time, a significantly underweight, eating disordered patient will often fly under the radar. While I understand that motivation from one's doctor can help reverse potentially harmful trends like inactivity, a flip side to doctorly advice exists. As sociologist Dr. Abigail Saguy of UCLA has pointed out in *What's Wrong with Fat?*, "In cases in which a patient has struggled and failed to lose weight, being told that her or his body size is inherently pathological can be harmful."[21]

I'm not saying that consistently eating more than your body needs, eating a diet of highly processed foods, and being sedentary aren't problematic—they are. But a portion of overweight and obese people are doing none of these behaviors, and they're still being condemned by their doctors, family and friends, and the culture at large.

If fat really isn't so bad, then why do we keep hearing the opposite message? If you turn on your TV or open a newspaper right now, you won't have to search long before finding a story about our obesity epidemic. Today, according to the BMI standards I described above, 69 percent of Americans (115 million) are considered overweight or obese. Worldwide, 1.4 billion adults and 40 million children under the age of 5 are overweight.[22] All of these people are in danger, we're told, because obesity is responsible for a host of serious illnesses, including cardiovascular disease, metabolic syndrome, and diabetes. Yet the studies I just presented to you show that these statements are grossly magnified.

Why, then, are advertisements, the media, and our own physicians telling us that we're in the midst of a crisis? Why do most of the news stories and articles we see right now focus on evidence that fat is bad instead of the equally convincing (often more statistically sound) evidence to the contrary that having some extra padding might reduce our disease mortality? Part of the issue is our cultural bias against fat. As I've discussed throughout this book, Americans have been moving toward a preference for greater and greater thinness for the past fifty years, accompanied by less tolerance for fat. Considering that "Fat active people have half the mortality rate of thin sedentary people," Paul Campos believes the "disease" of obesity could be a sociocultural construction designed to fuel bigotry against fat.[23] I tend to think he's right.

Marya Hornbacher, author of the eating disorder memoir *Wasted: A Memoir of Anorexia and Bulimia*, takes a look at health professionals. "Judging by the number of women I've talked to who have gone through hospital-setting treatment," she says, "it is fairly common to have nurses who have eating issues of their own."[24] Campos agrees. "Consider that anyone who attends a conference on the 'obesity epidemic' in America today is likely to find that a good number of the participants are extremely thin, high-achieving, upper-class white women, many of whom appear to have both strong perfectionist tendencies and a pathological fear and loathing of fat."[25] A number of therapists I've met through the years have had trouble enjoying what I'd call a normal meal. Mental health professionals are not immune to the culture at large. If we live in a culture that fears fat, populated by researchers and health professionals who also fear fat, yes, many of our research studies will begin with the hypothesis that fat is bad.

However, a biased medical community can account for only so much. The real reason the disease of obesity is suddenly an epidemic is that the war on this disease has individual, institutional, and corporate backing. As Gina Kolata points out in *Rethinking Thin*, a lot of people have a lot to lose if we to continue to show that being fat is not consistent with the dire health

BMI WHY?

If world-class athletes are overweight or obese according to their BMI, then maybe our gold standard for good health isn't so golden, after all. Is there a better way to measure our body size as it pertains to health? In a study published in *The Lancet*, researchers found that waist-to-hip ratios were better prognostic indicators of cardiovascular health and suggested we redefine obesity based on this ratio. Still, any health measurement that comes down to a single number is a blunt tool—a rough estimate that ignores a person's unique biology.[26]

consequences the media and diet industry would like us to believe. When it comes to research studies, the economics, politics, and even emotions of obesity garner more attention than the actual science of obesity.[27]

Kolata sums up the current situation like this: "I'd like to think also that as the population gets fatter, there might be a rethinking of the risks of a few extra pounds. When health data have not supported the alarmist cries of a medical disaster in the making, could society perhaps let up on the beleaguered fat people?"[28]

Fat Shaming: The Scapegoating of Heavy People

When did "fat" and "big" become such ugly words?

I remember attending a Broadway show once with a friend. In between numbers, I whispered to her something about one of the cast members.

"Which one?" she asked.

"The big one," I replied.

She looked at me curiously. "I'm surprised you said that," she said, all too familiar with my work. The show went on, as did our hushed dialogue.

"Why?" I asked. "I didn't mean it negatively. I was just trying to identify her."

In a sea of tiny, ballerina-bodied cast mates, the "big" one (probably a size 12) stood out. I could have said, "The one with the long black hair" or referred to the part she was playing, but this was honestly the first thing that came to mind, and when you're talking during a Broadway show, brevity is key.

To me, there's nothing wrong with referring to someone as "big," or "fat," or "large." They're descriptors and, taken alone, are judgment free. I much prefer these to "obese" or "overweight," which are relative terms and defined by BMI. I realize that not everyone agrees with me. Somewhere along the way, fat acquired a negative connotation. Now it's often used as a label, in a critical, mean-spirited way.

Fat and size is a touchy subject. While culturally we've made strides—at least in theory—with discrimination based on race and sexual orientation, fat is one area where overtly discriminating is still acceptable. It's almost as if our culture has channeled some of its previous biases toward other groups into this still politically correct form of prejudice. This prejudice, according to *Weight Bias at Home and School*, a video released by the Yale Rudd Center for Food Policy & Obesity, can be "as hurtful and difficult to counter as racial prejudice." The video goes on to list characteristics that people commonly attribute to those who are fat: "lazy," "stupid," "ugly," "unhappy," "unpopular," "mean," "greedy," and "gross."[29]

Ouch.

In 2008, the same group at Yale published a study in the *International Journal of Obesity*, suggesting that weight and height discrimination in women is as popular as racial discrimination and more popular than discrimination based on sexual orientation, ethnicity, or religion. The study also found that women may be discriminated against based on size at significantly lower weights than men. (In other words, men are allowed a little pudge.)[30] Another study showed that even if women do lose weight, they may still be judged for being heavy in the past.[31]

Sorry, ladies—there's no forgiving or forgetting.

Why do we judge heavier women like this? Many of us, it seems, perceive overweight women as failures, unsuccessful at managing even their own bodies. In her memoir, *Fat Girl: A True Story*, Judith Moore shares how it feels to be aware of this stereotype from her perspective on the receiving end. "When a thin person looks at a fat person, the thin person considers the fat person less virtuous than he. The fat person lacks willpower, pride, this wretched attitude, 'self-esteem,' and does not care about friends or family because if he or she did care about friends or family, he or she would not wander the earth looking like a repulsive sow, rhinoceros, hippo, elephant, general wide-mawed [sic] flesh-flopping flabby monster."[32]

The negativity and shaming heaped upon heavy people is not only cruel, it's also unfair—and based on false understandings of what fat means. Everything we know about obesity suggests that it is a complex phenomenon influenced by genetics and biology, as well as our food-rich environment. Personal responsibility isn't as great as it seems, yet we continue to blame fat people for their weight, convinced that they can control their bodies but choose not to. In truth, many obese people, like Moore, try and fail all the time to lose weight. "I am almost always on a diet," she says. "I hate myself. I have almost always hated myself. I have good reasons for hating myself, but it's not for bad things I've done.... I hate myself because I am not beautiful. I hate myself because I am fat."[33]

It's sad enough that fat shaming causes adult women like Moore to internalize this level of self-hatred. Now we're going a step further by blaming our nation's children. A 2012 campaign in Georgia, Strong4Life, targeted childhood obesity and raised alarm in the eating disorder community by depicting heavy children in a negative light. One ad showed a girl with a warning that read, "Fat kids become fat adults." Another image featured a boy with a caption that said, "Big bones didn't make me this way. Big meals did." Though the campaign was intended to be helpful and health-oriented, it focused more on body size than on the promotion of healthy eating and exercise behaviors. This type of ad is an example of the kind of negative, shaming messaging that, rather than being constructive, could actually encourage the development of eating disorders in those who may have such tendencies.[34]

As if having to endure this sort of public ridicule and self-reproach weren't enough, the obese population is also being blamed for one of our planet's most harrowing crises—global warming. According to an article by Gina Kolata in *The New York Times*, researchers calculated that the extra gasoline costs used to transport our growing nation are about one billion gallons per year.[35] In a more recent article, Brookings Institution economists linked obesity to our economic and educational crises, as well, blaming them for increased medical costs, decreased work productivity, decreased performance in school, and increased transportation costs and fuel consumption.[36]

Well, if obese people aren't necessarily sicker than the rest of us, perhaps we need to appeal to the greater good to convince them to lose weight. Have the dramas of global warming and the economic downturn tipped the scales to the point where the obese population will finally have that a-ha moment—the personal turning point when sudden insight leads to miraculous weight-loss results?

Not really. As Judith Moore pointed out, and as I discussed earlier, even when heavy people want to lose weight, their attempts often fail. As Gina

Kolata notes in the article above, "It's not that the obese don't care. Instead, as science has shown over and over, they have limited personal control over their weight. Genes play a significant role, the science says."[37] By raising the stakes, stigmatizing heavier people, and blaming them for personal, environmental, and sociopolitical ills, we're not helping them to get thinner. On the contrary, they're more likely to eat in response to the stress. They may avoid doctors who will shame them for their weight, resulting in untreated medical conditions. Blaming a fat person for being fat is akin to yelling at a stuttering child. What do we expect is going to happen? Stigma creates stress, which can have a real impact on illness and disease over time.

The best way for us to support the heavy among us is to learn the facts and let the truth guide us to a more compassionate and balanced outlook. If you are overweight or obese by current BMI standards, or if you know someone who is, please remember these tips:

- Not every obese woman needs to lose weight for her health. If you are active and eat well, you may be perfectly healthy as you are.

- If you are in good health, no one has the right to suggest you lose weight—not your doctor, your concerned family and friends, nor absolute strangers.

- "You might want to lose some weight" usually means the person making the comment prefers you to reduce yourself to a size she or he finds acceptable. Challenge "acceptable."

Compassion is important, for yourself and others. Sometimes life will lead to weight gain. It happens. The following story from one of my readers, Deborah, is a good reminder of how doctors' comments can be unnecessarily stigmatizing.

> I've spent the last 20 years fighting my weight, up and down; it's really been a struggle. My younger sister, Natalie, seems to have lucked out in the genes department. She's always been just naturally thinner than me. Until recently... Natalie never really lost the weight after her last baby. She later took a stressful job, was carting around three kids, just coping with life, and all of a sudden, she's pretty big. Definitely overweight, maybe

borderline obese. Natalie is disappointed in her weight gain, but losing weight just isn't a priority for her. She told me, though, that she's dreading her annual ob-gyn visit because she just knows her doctor is going to make a comment about her weight. It's not like Natalie doesn't know she's gained.

Look, she's my sister, and I want her to be healthy and happy. But clearly she's not going to change her life overnight. I wish that doctors would look at the full picture. If Natalie could lose the weight, I'm sure she would. If everything else looks good at her doctor's visit, shouldn't that be enough? Why can't her doctor actually ask about her eating and exercise, rather than just commenting on the scale? I wish that doctors would do that with me, too, because the truth is, I eat well and I'm active, regardless of how the scale fluctuates.

We have a lot of work to do to correct misconceptions and harmful language about fat and obesity, but insights like this give me hope. Organizations like the Association for Size Diversity and Health (ASDAH) and community resources like Health at Every Size (HAES) are working hard to educate the public about what fat means and what it doesn't. I encourage you to visit their websites (included in the appendix) to learn more about their programs, which focus on "accepting and respecting the natural diversity of body shapes and sizes."[38] HAES in particular offers a list of principles that focus on healthful eating, life-enhancing physical activity, and general, well-rounded wellness. Their message is that all of us, fat or thin, can be healthier and learn to appreciate one another as we are.

I hope that by promoting these movements we can work toward a place of greater size acceptance and refocus our agendas and efforts so that when we do express concern about someone's health, it will be just that—concern for her health—and not a thinly veiled attempt to express disapproval of her weight. Fat, after all, is not as harmful to us as we are to each other. According to Kolata, Katherine Flegal of the Centers for Disease Control and Prevention noted, "Yes, obesity is to blame for all the evils of modern life, except somehow, weirdly, it is not killing people enough.... In fact, that's why there are all these fat people around. They just won't die."[39]

Conclusion

If obesity isn't killing us the way we think it is and our war on fat isn't necessary, then why do we, as women, persist in enrolling in this fight? By now you're aware of the cultural influences that surround us every day, telling us fat is bad. The media, the diet industry, the language we use to describe food and eating, and even the medical community all reinforce the misconception that there's something wrong with a woman who isn't thin (and furthermore, doesn't want to be thinner). Why do we believe this misconception? In chapter 6, I'll look closely at how we become susceptible to body hatred and disordered behaviors, starting from birth—and what this targeting does to us over time.

CHAPTER 6

%% Eating and Body Image Concerns Across the Life Span

At what age does a girl begin to review
her assets and count her deficient parts? . . .
At what age does the process begin,
this obsessive concentration on the minutiae
of her physical being that will occupy some portion
of her waking hours quite possibly for the rest of her life?
— SUSAN BROWNMILLER

AS AN INFANT, a friend's little girl had trouble keeping food down. Failing to gain weight, she was diagnosed with gastrointestinal reflux disease and eventually prescribed medication. As the medicine started to take its effect, the baby held on to her meals and began to gain weight, and celebrations of her newfound pudge ensued.

I realized, sadly, that this could be the last time in this girl's life that people would delight in her putting on weight. Too soon, any excess poundage would be accompanied by frowns, pity, and prescriptions to take it off. When she started school, adults would tell her she'd make friends a little more easily, get teased a little less frequently, and do better academically if she just lost some weight. As she got older, friends would insist that if she dieted, she'd have the boy/guy/man of her dreams. And, throughout her life, messages from the world around her would remind her, every day, that she's just 5 or 10 or however many pounds away from feeling better about herself. I wondered, looking at this beautifully round baby, if the rest of us would ever remember the time when we reveled in the chubbiness of her infant thighs.

As a woman, from the time you're born until the time you die, your body is a target: for observation, judgment, and speculation from others and yourself. This chapter explores a woman's rites of passage through childhood, adolescence, school, love, pregnancy, and old age, and how each of these stages of life is ripe with opportunities for you to increasingly discount your body and yourself.

Childhood/School Years

Have you ever spent time with a 2-year-old girl? She wants to perform for you, play dress-up, and parade around the house, often in various stages of undress—but not for long. Soon, she'll be introduced to cultural expectations about her body from parents, friends, classmates, and the media, all separating her from her connection to, and the joy she once felt from, her body. She might develop a disordered relationship with food or poor body image. Unfortunately, she will never be the same.

Losing Your Body Innocence and Becoming Body Aware

In the beginning, there was light, or so the story goes. But in *our* beginnings as women, there was darkness—perhaps a faint silhouette, but certainly not a mirror. Each of us was born with an unawareness of self, a naive innocence I call "body innocence." Body innocence has to do with knowing what your body can do, knowing what you look like, but not being "aware" of your body—not judging your appearance, not worrying about what you're eating, not checking yourself in the mirror, not weighing yourself repeatedly, and not using your clothing as an innovative metric. This unawareness is accompanied by cognitive innocence of all things diet and weight-related. Becoming body aware (versus innocent) does not necessarily lead to an eating disorder; however, body awareness is often the first step down a winding, insidious path.

When I begin working with new clients, I like to ask them, "How far back do you have to go to arrive at a time when you weren't aware of your body? Twelve years old? Ten? Four?" One woman answered, "I can't even remember a time." One of my blog readers wrote that she became aware of her body at age 6, when her best friend called another girl "totally fat." Another reader had her revelation at the schoolyard, when a whole group of children called her fat. Comments often come from family members; one reader made it to her teenage years before she became aware of her body as an object, courtesy of a comment from her brother while hanging out at the pool: "You can stand to lose a few pounds." From that point forward, she was aware of her weight, saying, "[I] haven't stopped thinking about my body since."

EXERCISE: Body Awareness

Can you recall a time that you weren't aware of your body? Think back to your childhood. Can you remember how it felt to be naked or in a swimsuit (or even clothed, for that matter) and *not* be aware of your body: to have built a sandcastle on the beach and focused on the sand and the tide, but not your dimpled thighs? To have run through sprinklers on a hot day, focused on the wet grass and your friends and the heat and the water, but not the wiggle in your arms? When you're fully in the moment, absorbed by a connection or a feeling, it's impossible to be completely focused on that and your body at the same time. Keep a log of these moments and try to re-create them.

Not every instance of body awareness is caused by an unkind comment. Some girls come to feel that smaller is better at school, when they're forced to stand in the back row for class photos because they're taller than other girls, or even some of the boys (and therefore, usually, heavier). This size comparison plays out elsewhere, such as family gatherings and at extracurricular activities. Other girls learn body awareness through sports or dance. Girls involved in weight-dependent sports and pursuits like dancing, gymnastics, and ice skating are especially prone to body smashing. One of my blog readers wrote that she became body aware around age 4, during her first ballet performance.

She worried about "being fatter than the other girls." Jenni Schaefer, author of *Life Without Ed*, shares, "I sat in a circle with the other girls in my dance class and listened to the instructor explain the importance of being thin. She told us how we should eat, and she taught us exercises that would help us tone those flabby parts of our bodies. I was only 7 years old."[1]

My own experience is similar. When I was eleven, in the car on the way to gymnastics practice, I looked over at my friend Sarah's seat belt and noticed that it lay more flatly across her lap than mine did. I saw that the slight rise of my abdomen was more pronounced than hers and that somehow—and this is key—this was bad. I'd picked up on this message, maybe from family members' comments about other peoples' bodies or from exposure to the 1980s' fitness craze, championed by Jane Fonda. Noticing my body in relation to my friend's was my personal indoctrination to the world of body image, one in which every woman can judge her body against every other's.

Ten Body Awareness Triggers

What causes us to lose our body innocence—to become, in my words, "body aware"? Based on my research and my conversations with blog readers, I developed a list.

1. An unsuspecting comment by a family member, friend, or peer
2. A purposely cruel comment by a family member, friend, or peer
3. Losing some weight unintentionally and being consequently reinforced by others
4. Realizing ourselves that we're not as skinny as other children
5. Being involved in a weight-dependent activity, such as ballet, gymnastics, cheerleading, or ice-skating (let's not even say "figure skating")
6. Exposure to constant media messages about unnaturally thin celebrities
7. Exposure to constant media messages about the dangers of being overweight
8. Exposure to constant media messages that promote diet pills, plans, and procedures

9. Exposure to family members, friends, or peers who aren't body innocent

10. Abuse

Several of the above are demonstrated poignantly in the Oscar-nominated film *Little Miss Sunshine*, which is about an average 7-year-old girl who decides to compete in a beauty pageant. In the film, young Olive orders waffles a la mode at a restaurant. As she ponders the small dish of chocolate ice cream before her, her father persuades her to abstain by citing qualitative statistics about how pageant contestants don't eat ice cream. Dejectedly but resolutely, Olive resists.

When she finally arrives at the Little Miss Sunshine pageant, she prepares for her swimsuit and talent competitions. Looking around, she notices she is unlike the other prepubescent participants. Her hair isn't hot-iron curled, her body isn't blasted with fake tanner, her makeup is subtle, and her mother is comparatively unobtrusive. In one of the saddest scenes of the film, Olive pauses in front of the mirror and seems to catch her reflection for the first time. As she self-consciously evaluates her childlike frame, you can almost read her mind. She's noticing she's a bit pudgier than the other girls, and she's probably grateful she didn't indulge in that ice cream. Olive looks at her reflection with a disappointment that can only reflect the internalization of adult-like messages. It's a moment that signifies hope shattered, innocence lost, all in a pregnant gaze.[2]

Most of us, like Olive, have been exposed to at least one of the triggers on the above list, and yet genetically or temperamentally we remain insulated against anorexia, bulimia, or binge-eating disorder. However, what we're not protected from are the self-evaluation and self-attack that result from experience with the above factors. These early influences sting when they occur and can leave a lasting impression. For many of us, the moment lives on for the rest of our lives. For some, a predisposed biology works in concert with these influences to lead to the development of a full-blown clinical eating disorder. One of my blog readers wrote in with her story about the body awareness moment that set her on the road to anorexia. When she was just a preschooler, she witnessed her mother getting out of the bath, slapping at her fat and commenting about her "Jell-O butt." Years later, hospitalized to treat her eating disorder, she encircled her thigh with her hands and "flashed back to that memory."

Raising a Daughter to Have Healthy Relationships with Food and Her Body
As women, we cannot assume that our negative feelings about our own bodies aren't being communicated to our daughters, little sisters, students, or other young girls in our lives. Even if you never criticize a child for her appearance, by observing and imitating the behavior you model, she may still be getting the message that something is wrong with the way she looks. If you diet, glance slyly at your rear end in the mirror, or have a morning ritual of stepping on the scale, your daughter will see that and make note of it. Without saying a word, your actions communicate something crucial to her: thinner is better, and any shape that does not conform is unacceptable. No matter how much love you give her, if you dislike your own body, she will likely do the same.

But what if your child really is overweight or headed in that direction? Shouldn't you step in and try to help before it's too late and the problem gets out of control? Some mothers (fathers, too) feel that the best way to help their daughters, living as we are in a world that is unkind to heavier people, is to be proactive about weight management. I know of mothers who weigh their daughters, restrict their food, and buy them diet pills. Some mothers, like writer Pam Houston's used to do, shout advice like "Hold your tummy in!" for all the children on the school bus to hear.[3]

Others will purchase new wardrobes for their daughters following a significant weight loss, even if accomplished via an eating disorder. But does this type of parental involvement help or hurt the growing girl? (I think you can guess at my answer.)

The Showtime TV series *Weeds* depicts an ongoing mother-daughter weight struggle that you've probably seen, in less drastic form, in real life. Mother Celia Hodes (Elizabeth Perkins) worries about her daughter's "husky" size, so she regularly weighs Isabelle (played by 12-year-old Allie Grant). When Isabelle gains weight, Celia accuses her of sneaking food. Isabelle denies this. When Celia finds a chocolate bar in her daughter's room, she sneakily swaps part of it for a chocolate laxative. Later, Isabelle runs into the elementary school bathroom, the flatulent target of her peers. When she gets home, Isabelle's father yells at Celia, "They called her 'Shit Girl!'"

"Well, better than 'Fat Girl,'" the mother replies to her husband. "It is cold and cruel out there for fat girls."

Overhearing this, Isabelle plots her revenge by planting Imodium in Celia's Trimspa bottle, rendering her mother bloated, constipated, and enraged. As Celia makes camp on the toilet, reading, doing a crossword puzzle, filing her nails, chugging water, and even nodding off, Isabelle sits in bed, happily polishing off a chocolate bar.[4]

Was Isabelle actually hungry at this point? Was it really about the chocolate bar? Maybe, or maybe she ate out of rebellion, just to show she could. Children of excessively strict parents may soothe themselves with food in an effort to comfort themselves following (or preceding) frequent disciplining. In a system where rigidity is key, children like Isabelle may rebel by overeating, sneaking food as an effort toward self-expression or separation from the family.

This war between Celia and Isabelle only slightly exaggerates a common body struggle I've observed between mothers and daughters. Aware of our society's bias against fat, concerned mothers (and fathers, too) will often judge, criticize, or even control their daughters' food intake to insulate them from potentially more critical bystanders. The instinct is protective, but the irony is that this strategy doesn't work. A study conducted by Boston University's School of Medicine, appearing in the June 2006 issue of *Pediatrics*, revealed that children of authoritarian (strict disciplinarian) mothers are more than four times more likely to be overweight by the first grade than those reared by more authoritative (democratic) mothers (and also more likely to be overweight than those raised with permissive or neglectful parenting styles). Why would kids raised by overly strict mothers tend to be more overweight than those exposed to more flexible parenting? The researchers suggest that authoritarian parents may inhibit children from developing their self-regulatory abilities, which might result in their "learning to eat on the basis of external rather than internal cues." They posit that children raised in homes where exercise is mandated may lose their inherent interest in physical activity. Even more, the authors suggest that children may overeat as a "stress response" to parenting that is overly regimented and has unrealistic demands for self-control.[5]

One of my readers, Jillian, grew up in such a household. In preschool and kindergarten, her parents packed granola bars and raisins for her to eat during snack time, rather than allowing her to eat the cookies and punch her school provided. When her mother did give her permission one day to eat some cookies with the other kids, she filled her mouth with them, saying, "I held on to the mortar-like mix for as long as I could because I never knew when I'd get another cookie again." Jillian's mother sent her to friends' parties carrying a banana that she was allowed to eat instead of birthday cake.

She remembers going to an aquarium with her family when she was 11. "My cousins complained that they were hungry, and their father ushered off to the concession stand to pick up some snacks. I was hungry, too, but wouldn't dare say a word because my father had already judged, 'They just eat whenever they want,' highlighting their weakness, their humanity. They eat when they're hungry. Imagine that." Jillian's favorite and most memorable days were sleepovers at her friends' houses, where, outside of her parents' view, she ate bowl after bowl of Lucky Charms cereal, noting, "I had a deficit to address." Her parents' rigidity around food caused Jillian to develop an unhealthy relationship with it. By the time she got to high school, she was alternately restricting, overeating, and overexercising, problems she struggled with into adulthood.

Excessive food control at a young age may not even help weight loss, and as in the example above, it often backfires. In any case, nothing thwarts the schoolyard bullies. Studies show that early body weight and shape awareness can create and perpetuate assaults on girls' developing self-esteem. According to a 2010 study based out of Pepperdine University, preschoolers as young as 3, provided with images of different-sized figures, demonstrated a clear preference for thinner shapes and an aversion to fatter ones. The girls consistently preferred thin girls for potential playmates or best friends. During a round of Candy Land or Chutes and Ladders, when asked to switch their game piece from a thin one to a fat one, many refused to switch and some stated, "I don't want to be her. She's fat and ugly." Or "I hate her because she has a fat stomach." On average, the girls assigned 3.1 negative terms (such as "mean," "stupid," "has no friends," "sloppy," "ugly," "loud") and 1.2 positive terms (including "nice," "smart," "has friends," "neat," "cute," "quiet") to describe fat figures, compared with an average of 1.2 negative and 2.7 positive adjectives for thin figures. Worried parents are right to be concerned—the world isn't kind to fat girls. However, preschoolers certainly don't come into these opinions on their own.[6]

How can you work to counteract this negativity and help your daughter love her body as it is? For starters, I recommend not using family time to watch TV programs like *The Biggest Loser*. Liz Vaccariello, editor-in-chief of *Prevention* magazine, once answered a reader question about whether or not to watch the popular weight-loss program with kids as young as five. Her response:

> Tragic! Five years old is too young to worry about her body. But then this controversial light bulb went on in my head: *The Biggest Loser* should be mandatory viewing in grade schools! And every mom should watch with her children.... To me, [*The Biggest Loser*] is a crystal clear message to kids that it's a WHOLE lot harder to lose the weight than it is to make an effort, every day, to keep from gaining in the first place.[7]

If you're truly interested in teaching healthy living to your daughter, why not enlist her help in the kitchen or take her on a walk outside or pass around a soccer ball, rather than sitting watching fat people try to lose weight (an activity that encourages fat shaming) in destructive, unhealthy ways?

To promote good health and help your daughter accept her body regardless of its size, I recommend you focus on teaching her healthy eating for health's sake rather than for potential weight outcomes. You should also focus on self-acceptance (your own as well as your daughter's), positive communication, and promoting physical activity for the right reasons—fun and health.

I shared the following list of positive actions with readers of my blog. While these tips won't eliminate eating disorders completely, particularly given the more we learn about genetic influences, they can help harness less clinically significant presentations and will certainly assist all of our girls in developing more positive relationships with food and their bodies.

5 Tips for Raising a Daughter to Have Healthy Relationships with Food and Her Body, by Dr. Stacey

1. Throw out your scale.

2. Talk about foods with regard to how they can nourish her body rather than their effects on her weight.

3. Encourage physical activity for the sake of health rather than weight control.

4. Don't judge your body in front of her. Don't say negative things about your body or even glance in the mirror in a critical way.

5. Focus on all of her strengths outside of her body, but make it a point to tell her how beautiful she is.

It turned out my readers, many of whom were mothers and all of whom were daughters, had their own suggestions to add.

Six More Tips, by Dr. Stacey's Readers

1. Understand that you're a role model for your daughter. Avoid "fat talk" about others as well as yourself.

2. Refrain from labeling foods as "good" or "bad"; don't ban any foods; encourage your daughters to eat when they're hungry and stop when they're full.

3. Recognize the power that the media has and either limit or discuss the reality of television shows, magazines, and so on, with your daughter.

4. Select doctors for your children that value health over weight.

5. Promote body diversity in your home.

6. Understand that even with the best intentions, your daughter may still go on to develop disordered eating. Educate yourself about signs and symptoms

of eating disorders. Provide unconditional love and
support, as well as access to good treatment.

What a thorough and helpful list! If only all moms could heed this advice.

When I talked to Leslie Goldman, author of *Locker Room Diaries*, she highlighted a valuable tip about introducing young girls to locker rooms and changing areas in preparation for gym classes and sports or dance activities in the future. She suggests that you avoid the scale, keep the talk focused on accomplishments, and, most important, "Do not point out flaws in your own body. Make a concerted effort not to grimace at your body as you look in the mirror, or as you tweeze your eye brows.... Don't focus on looking at yourself in the mirror. Make it a time when the two of you can have mother-daughter time and not a body-bashing session."[8]

Raising a daughter is never easy. Goldman's advice shows just how vigilant all women need to be if we hope to be positive role models for girls. By deemphasizing appearance in general, however, you can go a long way toward helping your daughter mature in an environment where she feels her primary value comes from who she is and not how she looks.

Parents, of course, are not the only influences on girls. These days, the obesity crisis puts children's bodies under a microscope, sometimes even more so than their brains. I know a number of teachers and educators who have encouraged weight loss among their students, some even going so far as to assign school-aged children homework to lose weight, tracking their results as part of a class project.

What can you do, as a mother or mentor to girls, to combat these negative influences outside the home?

1. Get involved at your child's school. Make sure that teachers aren't giving weight-loss assignments to your child's class. Some schools now measure students' BMIs, an effort that is ill focused and can shame heavier students. Fight back and encourage the school to add programming that focuses on health, not weight.

2. Get to know your daughter's friends. Spend time with them and model flexible eating and healthy exercise. Encourage pursuits with girls that are activity- rather than beauty-oriented (e.g., a bowling outing, rather than a makeup session).

3. Talk with your daughter about bodies in the media and advertising. Educate her early about the unrealistic nature of the images she sees.

4. Ask her about conversations and messages she hears about weight and size. Encourage her to think critically about weight stigma.

Adolescence to College

Adolescence poses a unique set of body image challenges. Fresh from the physical and psychological provocation of puberty, many girls find themselves in hypercompetitive academic, social, and extracurricular environments, where dieting and perfectionism take center stage. Then, as they leave the nest, teens confront additional tests around food and weight, often on the scene of college campuses.

Puberty and the "Supergirl"

In today's ubercompetitive environment, some kids, or at least their parents, start thinking about college applications as soon as preschool. In response, girls feel increasing pressure to excel academically, athletically, and socially. Unfortunately, their bodies become another dimension of this drive for success. Liz Funk, the teenage author of *Supergirls Speak Out: Inside the Secret Crisis of Overachieving Girls*, knows a thing or two about this phenomenon. "In the seventh grade, I set my sights on Harvard and wanted to achieve academically. So I studied and got on the high honor roll....I became editor of the school newspaper, joined the foreign cultures club....In the ninth grade, I became obsessed with my size and my looks, and I ended up becoming anorexic."[9]

Soon, Funk was pushing herself to run several miles a day with the cross-country team. When she gained back weight she lost—a natural part of puberty—she pushed herself harder.

Like Funk, many girls internalize from a fairly young age that being super involves being skinny. Pressure to succeed comes from every direction: teachers, guidance counselors, fellow students, coaches, friends, and romantic interests. Sometimes a girl's body can take the brunt of this stress. Some turn to disordered eating as a way to cope with the many rigors of growing up a girl.

What can you do to support your daughter so she doesn't slip into self-reproach? Funk suggests we pay closer attention to how girls respond to stress. "While we should be totally supportive of the go-getter young women, we need to be cognizant of the girls whose assiduousness becomes an obsession, where 100 isn't good enough, and overachieving eventually becomes an addiction. Or a mental disorder."[10]

Warning signs: If you (or a girl in your life) cannot tolerate imperfection, get rattled at the smallest signs of failure, get obsessed with performing and succeeding, often at the expense of just being a girl (spending time with friends, sleeping, daydreaming), then you may be on your way to a problem.

As if growing up weren't difficult enough, prepubescent girls enter early adolescence with a set of biological stressors, as well. Developing bodies, including growing breasts, stomachs, butts, hips, and legs, result in inevitable weight gain. It's not uncommon for a girl to gain 20 percent of her body weight (in fat) during puberty. At exactly the time that a girl has cemented in her mind that she must be thin to be accepted by her peers, she is gaining uncontrollable amounts of weight. It's not surprising, then, that dieting and disordered eating behavior increases during this time of transition, often among friends. One large study found that female adolescents who had friends who dieted were more likely to engage in chronic dieting, unhealthy weight-control methods, and binge eating several years down the road.[11]

Stories abound of girls dieting together, body bashing together, and even bingeing and purging together. For example, Kaley's first experience with food restriction occurred during her teenage years. A student in New York City, she would leave the school for lunch and patronize nearby pizza shops and delis for lunch with her friends. One year, Kaley's best friend suggested they start going to the local Starbucks instead. The girls drank coffee instead of eating a solid lunch and enjoyed the adult-like nature of their outings, as well as their collective weight loss over time. "It didn't seem disordered at the time," Kaley reflects back. "But it's the first time I skipped meals, and I wonder if I would have done it on my own."

Because they are working against the biology of their growing bodies, these efforts at weight control often fail, or are temporarily successful but result in overeating later on, as compensation for prior restriction.

Social Media

Body scrutiny during childhood, tween, and teen years has been complicated recently by a new trend that didn't exist before the millennium: social media. In my practice over the last ten years, I've noticed a dramatic increase in concerns about body image related to the Internet and cell phones. In the past, if someone snapped a picture of you at a party, the picture would just be shared among friends. Now, due to the explosion of social media and texting—especially among kids and teens—pictures can be shared with thousands of friends on different social networking sites. Within Facebook, for example, an unflattering or unapproved photo may end up on a friend's time line, tagged with your name, where it's then archived for eternity (or until your friend relents and takes it down or untags you). This wider, almost infinite, audience increases concerns about body image in women of all ages. It's not uncommon for me to hear women state that they plan to avoid a social event altogether for fears that pictures will be posted online.

The Freshman 15

During childhood and adolescence, girls are exposed to thousands of messages about staying thin to fit in, both offline and online. By the time a young woman approaches college, she is often firmly entrenched in our dieting culture. Some have already met criteria for clinical eating disorders

---

IS SOCIAL MEDIA MAKING YOU ANTISOCIAL?

How do you feel when unflattering photos of you turn up online? Do you ignore them? Ask the poster to remove them? Do you go a step further and ask people not to take your picture, or do you even stay home from an event? If you're with friends or at an event and having a good time and a cell phone picture is snapped, can you try to remind yourself, it's not about the picture? If you see an unflattering photo of yourself online, can you take a deep breath and move on?

by this point, and a host of others dislike their bodies and fear weight gain of any kind.

Then they learn about the freshman 15, those dreaded 15 pounds of weight that college students often put on during their first year away from home. A 2003 study at Cornell University explored the freshman 15 phenomenon, finding that on average, first-year students gained just over 4 pounds during their first twelve weeks on campus.[12] This sudden change, though small, can be stressful to young women who've already spent years of their lives dieting.

Though a temporary weight gain of this manner is hardly a public health issue or a matter that would affect one's studies, often universities respond to weight-gain fears by cautioning students about contributing factors and informing them of what they can do to avoid or counter weight gain. Cornell posted such a list on its Health Services website, naming a series of common student behaviors (for example, staying up late, eating from vending machines, and drinking alcohol) as factors that may lead to gaining weight. Much of this is reasonable nutritional advice; however, some sounds similar to the language on pro-ana sites ("eat slowly and sip water with your meals"), and the parting shot sounds unnecessarily alarmist:

> Check your weight occasionally and notice any trends. If you observe a consistent increase over several weeks, or if you notice that you are overeating to cope with stress, consider an appointment with the Cornell Healthy Eating Program. Don't obsess, but if you've tried the suggestions above and need some help, it might be time to talk to a nutritionist or other health professional. It's better to address any weight issue before it becomes a bigger problem.[13]

The thing is, the freshman 15 isn't going to kill anyone, but becoming hyperfocused on weight at exactly the time that you're putting on a few pounds could be the exact combination that triggers something dangerous.

For the most part, this is a predictable byproduct of leaving behind the structured life of high school. College is the first time young women are on their own, free from the monitoring of helicopter parenting. It's the first time that they may have free rein to restrict or overeat, without constant watch from teachers and parents. They likely aren't getting adequate sleep, and they're probably drinking more than they did before. College can also be a demanding time, full of academic, social, and identity-based stressors. Young women, now independent, are figuring out who they are and what they want. It's not surprising, then, that eating disorders flourish on campuses. National research shows that the average age of onset for an eating disorder is 18 to 21 years, right in the middle of a woman's college years.[14]

Greek Life: Sororities and Fraternities

For those women who opt to participate, university Greek life can amplify disordered thoughts or behaviors. Many sororities favor admitting thin, attractive women to boost the status of their organizations. Fraternities, in turn, cosponsor parties with high-status sororities and hand select pretty underclass women to attend or hostess (a selection that is deemed to be an honor). In this world, beauty becomes social capital, and thinness becomes the key to acceptance by both men and other women. One fraternity at American University in Washington, DC, printed up T-shirts that read on the front, "Please don't feed the sorority girls," and on the back, "Campus beautification," along with the fraternity's letters.[15]

You might not be surprised to learn that eating disorders are common in sororities, but they can even be condoned and encouraged through a spirit of camaraderie. In *The New York Times* bestseller *Pledged: The Secret Life of Sororities*, Alexandra Robbins goes undercover among a group of sorority members to expose the inner workings of female Greek groups. She soon learns about "Pig Runs," when newly selected sorority members ("pigs") sprint to the Greek houses that choose them. She also discovers the importance of gym attendance. "Gymming had become a popular gerund [in sororities], as in, 'I need to go gymming if I eat this cookie.'"[16] Size, of course, is the ultimate membership card. She reports, "One sister was dropped from the school's cheerleading squad because she was too fat...a size 2."[17]

According to *Rush: A Girl's Guide to Sorority Success*, a manual that Robbins quotes in her book, women's bodies are of major importance to the sorority selection process. Not having much to go on besides looks, sorority members rate rushees after just several minutes of conversation. Looking good can carry a woman further in the process. "For example, if you are overweight, you must try to lose weight before rush. If you have acne problems, you should work on clearing up your face. Whatever problems you have, you must do your best to minimize them. Physical attractiveness plays a large part in the overall evaluation process."[18]

I've seen this process firsthand. When I was in a sorority, we were instructed to rate each rushee on a scale of 1 to 5, shouting out the numbers in front of the entire sisterhood to debate the pros and cons of each applicant. Having sat through this process for one year, I was happy to be abroad the next. How can you rate a person on a 1 to 5 scale? It's not hard, according to some. A visitor from our national office rhetorically asked us, "You don't want any dogs in the house, do you?"

Once selected, many sorority women continue to be subjected to scrutiny. As Robbins says in her book:

> During circle the fat, pledges undress and, one by one, stand in front of the entire sorority membership. The sisters (or, in some chapters, fraternity brothers) then use thick black markers to circle the fat or cellulite on a pledge's body. The purpose is to help the pledge learn what parts of her body she needs to improve.... During bikini weigh, or "weigh-in," pledges are weighed in front of either the sisterhood or a fraternity; the audience yells the number displayed on the scale.[19]

Thankfully, these practices did not occur in my house, but that doesn't mean that eating disorder behaviors were absent. It's no wonder that plumbers must frequently service sorority houses, as Robbins notes, to unclog the vomit-ravaged pipes. In an overall university environment, where eating disorders are rampant, disordered behaviors flourish, perhaps to an even greater degree, in sororities that maintain such practices and expectations.

When I returned from my semester abroad my junior year, I took a leave from my sorority my senior year. For those who choose to remain active in their houses, the body-bashing environment may be to them just part of the devil's bargain to be Greek, may not seem so different from messages they get from society at large, or may confirm negative ideas they already have about their bodies.

Of course, not every young woman at college participates in the Greek system, but sororities are a microcosm of the university community as a whole (and, arguably, the adult world outside of college): an environment in which relative attractiveness may predict social success, professional networking, and romantic success and desirability.

Adulthood

You might think that by the time a woman transitions out of adolescence and begins to live life on her own, she'd shed her teenage concerns around food and weight. Think again. Young women are confronted with body image challenges as they date and mate, marry, and get pregnant and have children. A woman's body, miraculously capable of growing and nourishing another human being, is still judged as just a body.

Dating

Though I don't mean to start a gender war on these pages, it must be said: a host of additional body image concerns present themselves as women enter the heterosexual dating world (note that I invoke a heterosexist assumption here and that same-sex relationships may present similar or different concerns). Because we're taught from birth that thin equals beautiful, those of us who are straight understand that to attract and maintain the attention of a man, we must lose weight or maintain a slim figure. I've heard this concern over and over again from the women I see in my practice. Dating and sex are among the top causes of body anxiety in women, and is it any wonder, given what some men seem to be looking for? Witness these three singles ads, which I found on a widely used Internet dating site. One bachelor stated a preference for "thin or small girls." Another had a more specific body type in mind, asking that his potential dates be "curvy" but not "fat," with "slim waists contrasted by curves up top and down below." A final bachelor requested someone "extremely thin and dainty" and then just came out and said it: "on the anorexic side."

You may not believe what I'm about to say, but it's true: behind every man seeking anorexic bliss is someone alarmingly insecure. In selecting a frail, fragile, disappearing girl, he's hoping to overpower, overcome, and outweigh his mate, while at the same time impressing the crowds by being seen with a model ideal. Is this really someone you'd want to date—someone who needs you to be smaller so he can feel bigger?

EXERCISE: Flip the Gaze

The next time you try Internet (or real-world) dating, try not to think about what a man or mate may want in you. Instead, assume you have a lot to offer and focus on what qualities you can expect from him.

Remember, many men are looking for women with natural, healthy bodies, women who bring more to the table than the size of their waists and the clarity of their bones. I have known men who desire women who are smart, funny, patient, considerate, adventurous, ambitious, loving, or maternal. There is so much more to partner preference than size. For every woman who's sat in my office and told me that she must lose weight to find love and happiness, I'll tell her about the skinny women I know who are single and unhappy and the fat women I've encountered who are euphorically in love.

Some men will want to date models, but plenty don't, and for good reason—biology doesn't support a desire for a rail-skinny mate. Research has shown that across cultures, men prefer one feature of a woman's body over all others—a waist-to-hip ratio that hovers at 0.7. This ratio means that the circumference of one's waist measures approximately 70 percent the circumference of her hips (think classic Marilyn Monroe hourglass). Research shows that men's neural reward centers fire when viewing pictures of women with hourglass shapes.[20] Even blind men, never exposed to media ideals about women's bodies, prefer women with a certain waist-to-hip ratio.[21] Men seem to be wired to find a curvier body—specifically, around the hip area—more attractive. Apparently, storing weight around the hips and butt may be an evolutionary indicator of fertility; one study found that as the waist-to-hip ratio increased, rates of fertility (conception) decreased.[22]

Now, before you take out your tape measure, think about all the medical and lifestyle contortions we consider or even undergo to appeal to men— breast implants, liposuction, excessive exercise, and starvation diets. No research suggests that protruding clavicles, sternums, ribs, or hips are sexually attractive to men unless, because of their own psychology, they're looking for a little girl. Even the perfect waist-to-hip ratio is a fraction, not an individual.

Regardless of what men do or don't want, dating for the average, curvy, or heavy woman can be fraught with self-esteem perils, sometimes from unexpected directions. Once, Liz Funk, author of *Supergirls Speak Out*, interviewed me for an online magazine article. She asked if overweight women might miss out on sexual opportunities and how these women might become more comfortable with sex. I stand by my answer from the article: "There are plenty of women who are fat who are in great relationships and plenty of women who are thin and dating unsuccessfully. Women should be focusing on the things they bring to a relationship other than just their looks."[23]

Marriage and Weddings

If you're single, you may be thinking, *When I find the perfect person, I'll be able to relax and let my stomach out.* Weddings, however, can be fraught with body image anxiety for any woman, particularly for those with preexisting eating problems. In an article in a 2009 issue of *Brides* magazine, Abby Ellin writes about the happily betrothed (many who are already quite thin) taking extreme measures to lose weight before their wedding days. Ellin, who interviewed me for the piece, covers an alarming trend that has become the norm: a world where the newly engaged are seduced into weight loss by smaller-than-average dresses, Facebook ads for diet plans and gowns (which appear the instant they change their status to "Engaged"), and pictures documenting every step of the ordeal—the promise of forever in print.[25]

The proliferation of bridal boot camps and TV shows like *Bulging Brides* and *Say Yes to the Dress* reinforce the idea that no matter how thin you are, to walk down the aisle, you must be thinner. Brides-to-be respond to this message, of course; you'd be hard pressed to find a bride who isn't doubling up on cardio classes or daily runs in the months or weeks before her wedding. One woman crammed for her wedding four weeks before by going to hour-long spinning classes daily and setting the tension knob at a ridiculously

IS "SEXY" RELATIVE?

In a 2009 study published in *Sex Roles*, researchers examined 5,810 Internet dating profiles and found that white men advertised more of a preference for thin and toned women, while African-American and Latino men demonstrated preferences for average, large, thick, or voluptuous female bodies.[24]

high resistance. When she almost fainted, her teacher asked her why she was pushing herself so hard. Her response, "My wedding is only four weeks away!"

According to a Brides.com poll Ellin quotes in her article, "Seventy-four percent of respondents said they were trying to lose more than 10 pounds for their wedding."[26] In another study Ellin references, "More than half of [the bridal dieters, many who resorted to extreme measures] were of normal weight to begin with."[27] Several of the brides, boot camp teachers, and wedding industry consultants quoted in the article talk about the frenzy to lose weight being worse than what we see just prior to bikini season. One woman Ellin quotes stated, "Every bride I know starved for her wedding." Most gain the weight back ("like the freshman 15," according to one bridal salon owner), but it's the thought of having the photos forever that haunts women into engaging in disordered and restrictive behavior in the months or weeks leading up to their big days.[28]

EXERCISE: Wedding Planning

Your wedding is about so much more than your body. If you go to unhealthy measures to lose weight before your big day, you might look thinner in your pictures (though not necessarily like yourself), but you'll likely gain the weight back plus some. Restricting and overexercising doesn't make for a happy bride. It just increases any stress you feel as the event approaches. Why not enjoy your engagement, your wedding, and the rest of your life by responding to hunger, eating with pleasure, and accepting yourself for who you are?

Pregnancy

If weddings are stressful times for women who worry about their weight, pregnancy may be an even more challenging test. What should be an exciting and beautiful time can often be bristling with worries about gaining too much or giving up regular workouts. I remember being at the gym one day when I saw a woman taking pregnancy photos clad in a sports bra and spandex short-shorts. She viewed the images and frowned. She looked at me, watching from the elliptical machine, and mouthed the words, "Back fat."

I shook my head. "Beautiful," I said.

Eyeing my elliptical machine, she responded, "I wish I could be doing that."

I got to thinking about how many women wish they could find suitable partners, wish they could get pregnant, wish they could have healthy babies, but this pregnant woman was wishing she could be working out, wishing her back would have less fat. Though I didn't agree with her self-assessment of how she looked, I understood how she felt and why she felt that way. Whether or not a woman has pre-existing body image concerns, she'll be put to the test with pregnancy. For those who struggled with food prior to pregnancy, these forty weeks can be exceptionally challenging. Morning sickness, weekly weight checks, a growing belly (and body despite a real and desired purpose), and sometimes well-intentioned comments about the "right" things to eat all can rile up an already shaky relationship with food and weight. Fertility treatments, on the rise, may also tack on additional prepregnancy gain.

As if the physical and emotional aspects of pregnancy aren't enough stress to bear, women's pregnant bodies are constantly scrutinized and judged by others, as I mentioned with regard to celebrities. Are you gaining enough weight? Are you gaining too much weight? Or are you the Goldilocks of motherhood? Remember also the weight patrol that hounds celebrities? The pregnancy patrol is similar. Women's pregnant bellies and bodies seem to be everybody's business.

Stop the Comments

In 2013, Internet magazine *Jezebel* ran an article lambasting the media hoopla around Kim Kardashian's pregnancy weight gain. They urged the media to "Shut the F--- Up" about her figure. We need to apply these words to every expecting mother. *Not one woman should be critically commenting on another woman's growing belly.* Doing so is the quickest, surest way to devalue the miracle of life.[29]

Why all of the commentary? Health reasons, of course.

According to a 2008 *New York Times* article entitled "Too Fat and Pregnant," gaining too much weight during pregnancy can be dangerous, especially for the already-fat demographic, who may be more likely to experience complications including hypertension and diabetes. Moreover, according to the article, the fetuses of fat women are often too large to navigate the birth canal, resulting in a higher incidence of cesarean sections. To combat these dangers, new crops of bariatric obstetric centers are advising fat patients to avoid gaining any weight during pregnancy, and maybe even to lose weight.[30]

Now, I might be a little presumptuous here, but if quick weight loss were possible, wouldn't the mother have done this already? How is it going to be any easier when she's with child? I wish that obstetricians would approach heavy pregnant women as individuals rather than statistics, looking at the health of each mother and baby, removed from body size. Doctors may encourage pregnant women to eat nutritious foods and exercise moderately because it's good for their pregnancies, but not because it's definitely going to result in rapid weight loss.

As it turns out, even thin women are sometimes given strict weight-related pregnancy recommendations by their doctors. A while back, Monica, a slim, pregnant friend of mine living in New York City, told me her obstetrician had issued some pretty strict guidelines about her pregnancy weight. Her doctor recommended she limit fruit to once or twice a week, avoid flour and other carbs, and not increase her calorie intake at all during the pregnancy. Monica said, "I was told not to eat any more than I was eating before I got pregnant since I looked 'normal' and 'thin' (prepregnancy). She said that the fetus does not need much in terms of calories." The ob-gyn recommended Monica gain no more than 25 pounds during pregnancy (though the standard medical recommendation is 25–35 pounds) because "any more is 'just weight you have to lose.'"

Monica did not appreciate her doctor's guidelines and considered switching to another obstetrician; the regular weigh-ins and pressure not to gain too much weight made her self-conscious during a time when she already had enough on her mind. When she gained 15 pounds during her second trimester, the doctor told her that since she had started the pregnancy thin, the gain was acceptable, but that if she'd been overweight to begin with and gained that much, she (the doctor) "would have been 'upset.'" In the end, Monica ended up eating as much fruit as she wanted, gained 22 pounds and lost it quickly, feeling relieved she would not disappoint her doctor during her postpartum checkups.

These days, the pressure to lose the baby weight is at an all-time high. Every day women are expected, like supermodels, to drop the baby weight and be runway ready within weeks of delivering. The serious work of getting one's body back often begins on the wheelchair ride out of the maternity ward. One of my readers commented that about twenty-four hours after giving birth, her hospital gave her a free diaper bag loaded with coupons, including one for Jenny Craig that featured the slogan, "Baby fat is cute...on a baby."

The diet companies know that women follow celebrity pregnancies closely. Famous women tend to drop baby weight relatively quickly, so you should, too (or so you're told). While some celebrities confess to rigorous diet or exercise plans, others often tell the media something to the effect of, "I'm breastfeeding; the weight has just disappeared" or "I'm running after her all day—it's been so easy to shed the pounds!" Whether or not these women are telling the truth doesn't matter; they perpetuate the myth that weight loss after baby is easy, and that isn't usually the case. Gaining the weight took time, and, thanks to biology, losing it will probably take even more time. Still, the public perception is that it's quick. If you can't lose baby weight fast, you simply aren't trying hard enough. Los Angeles–based writer Tracy Moore of the online magazine *Jezebel* found herself disappointed at how unforgiving the world is after a woman gives birth. She wanted to "get a minimum of five years' sympathy for weight gain after having a child, but it turns out that if Kate Hudson can exercise away her baby body in six months working out six hours a day, then you, average woman, should at least be able to do a coupla leg lifts in between burritos."[31]

Maturity: The Older Years

When you get older, finally you won't care about your belly or the size of your butt, right? You'll enjoy food and say "critics, be damned." Common legend is that older women don't exhibit disordered eating. Many women I've worked with, in fact, anticipate old age because they think that when they become older, they won't care about their bodies, their dissatisfaction will finally die down, and their eating problems (if they have them) will remit. When they're old, they think, their difficulties with emotional eating or overexercising will simply fade away.

But more and more research is suggesting the contrary—that signs of disordered eating and distorted body image are evident in the second half of life. A study of 1,849 women published by the *International Journal of Eating Disorders* in 2012 revealed that 13 percent of women ages 50 and older struggle with disordered eating. Other statistics were even more formidable: 36 percent of the women spent at least half of the last five years dieting, 41 percent said they scrutinized their body at least once a day, and more than 70 percent of the women surveyed said they were currently trying to lose weight.[32]

Carol is all too familiar with these statistics. Sixty-four, she still visits her bathroom scale daily and goes through phases where she restricts certain foods, like dairy, sweets, and bread. Fluctuating at most 20 pounds her whole life, Carol grew up in a family that valued appearance and, as an extension, thinness. As a result, she thinks, she has trouble accepting herself at the higher end of her weight range and becomes overly critical of certain body parts, particularly her stomach.

As she's aged, Carol has found it more challenging to keep weight off. It's frustrating and upsetting to her as she sees the number slowly creep up on the scale, and she tries to outsmart her biology by eating smaller meals. "It's odd how I've made peace with a lot of other things in my life, and I know that my weight doesn't really matter in the scheme of things, and I don't want it to matter, but I'm having trouble letting go of this one thing."

As women age, our beauty stock declines. Says psychology professor Joan Chrisler, "The point at which this happens no doubt differs for different women, but anecdotal evidence suggests that it is around 50 when women, particularly women who had previously been praised as beautiful, suddenly realize that no one is looking at them anymore."[33] It's this invisibility that may lead many aging women to cosmetic surgery.

With more and more women relying on medical enhancements to keep a youthful appearance, the bar has been raised for women of age. They, too, must look their best for as long as they can. Couple the availability of eternal youth with the fact that going through menopause often leads women to gain more than 10 pounds (as metabolism slows and estrogen production

OPPOSITE ACTION

You cannot and will not just grow out of an eating or body image problem. To feel better about yourself at any age, you must work to make active changes to improve your relationship with food and your body. I like to suggest the following exercise, one a 58-year-old reader of my blog credited for helping her finally accept her look as being healthy and attractive.

Borrowing a skill from dialectical behavior therapy, when you find yourself engaged in a moment of hatred toward your body, see if you can act opposite to this feeling. Instead of restricting or bingeing on food, weighing yourself, or body bashing in the mirror, think compassionate thoughts toward your body. For example, look in the mirror and instead of criticizing or listing flaws, think one good thought about the way you look. Other suggestions: Take a relaxing bath. Dress in comfortable clothing. Apply lotion to your legs. Get a massage. Enjoy sex. Have a satisfying meal. Acting opposite changes emotions over time and can send a radically different message to yourself about your body.

drops off), and it's not surprising that for many, the battle to get and stay thin and beautiful intensifies.

Conclusion

You're taught almost from birth to monitor your shape and size (and other women's, too). From your first awareness of your body through the life changes of puberty, sex, marriage, childbirth, and menopause, you're constantly focused on seeing yourself as flawed and 5 pounds too heavy (or more). How did things come to be this way? In chapter 7, I'll discuss some of the cultural foundations that have led us to the point where instead of enjoying our transformative life experiences, we're worrying—in the words of authors Claire Mysko and Magali Amadei—"Does this pregnancy make me look fat?"[34]

CHAPTER 7

⫻ Why Women?

*A cultural fixation on female thinness
is not an obsession about female beauty
but an obsession about female obedience.*
— NAOMI WOLF

MOST OF US KNOW WOMEN WHO STRUGGLE with body issues to some degree, but how many men do you know who spend an equal amount of time worrying about how their bodies look or how much space they take up? When I told people I was writing a blog and book called *Does Every Woman Have an Eating Disorder?*, the question "Why women?" inevitably surfaced. After all, both men and women go on diets. Both men and women overexercise. Men, increasingly, are closing the gap in disordered thinking and behaviors, particularly since binge-eating disorder became its own diagnosis and as our culture presses for a thinner, more muscular masculine ideal.

Still, the fact remains that anorexia and bulimia occur at significantly higher rates in women than in men, and even with cases of binge-eating disorder, women still occupy the majority.[1] Based on the clients my colleagues and I see in our practices, I can safely say that women are more commonly diagnosed with OSFED and make up the bulk of subclinical presentations, too (evidencing disordered behavior, but not necessarily a textbook disorder).

Why is this the case? Experts in the fields of psychology and gender studies have theories about the role of women in our culture, the role of our bodies in our lives, and why women are forced to justify our existence through our bodies. In this chapter, I'll look at these theories and examine how, as women, these concepts play out in our relationships with ourselves and one another.

A Woman's Body as Object

In the Wodaabe culture of West Africa, men compete in a seasonal pageant for the honor of most beautiful man. Aided by costumes, makeup, and body painting, they perform for a panel of judges. In a reversal from our own culture, Wodaabe women are their judges. Of course, I'm not suggesting that objectifying men is the answer to our societal problems, but I mention this example to highlight the cultural basis of judgment and desire. In our nation, women diet, spend thousands of dollars at hair salons, and apply makeup as if it's our civic responsibility, all toward the goal of presenting a more acceptable image to men and to the world. That we do this is not by any means natural or innate. It's simply a reflection of how we see women in Western culture (and many other cultures) at this point in time. How you are defined will largely be a reflection of how you look. Your body, therefore, is something to observe and discuss. Ask any woman and she will confirm this simple truth.

In her book *Femininity*, Susan Brownmiller asks this question about the everyday woman: "When is she allowed to forget that her anatomy is being monitored by others, that there is a standard of desirable beauty, of individual parts, that she is measured against by boyfriends, loved ones, acquaintances at work, competitors, enemies, and strangers?"[2] In our Western experience of gender and bodies, a woman's body exists as an object to be accepted or not, to be desired or not, to be trotted around on runways and pageant circuits and red carpets, and to advertise and market clothing. This idea is so ingrained in us that we hardly realize things might be different. Girls are socialized to be pageant contestants, models, pole dancers—their bodies front and center as commodities on display, their talents often hidden, their multidimensionality and whole selves left behind. Baby girls are paraded around in faux cheerleader uniforms for sports teams but less often in the team uniforms themselves. It's not surprising that girls grow up to understand their bodies to be of central value, to know their appearance to be more important than anything else.

In *Killing Us Softly 3*, author and documentarian Jean Kilbourne claims:

> Men and women inhabit very different worlds. Men basically don't live in a world in which their bodies are routinely scrutinized, criticized, and judged, whereas women do. Now, this doesn't mean that there aren't stereotypes that harm men. There are plenty of stereotypes that harm men, but they tend to be less intimate, less related to the body.[3]

Is it any wonder that with this emphasis on the body, women are more prone to disordered eating? In *Bulimia: A Guide to Recovery*, Lindsey Hall and Leigh Cohn describe several factors that make women more susceptible to eating disorders:

- "Women are socialized in ways that increase their risk of getting eating disorders."

- "Having a female body in this society can be frightening."

- "Our society denies the natural variety and function of women's bodies."

- "Women are expected to control their emotions."

- "Women are frustrated in the workplace."

- "The media and money perpetuate the status quo."[4]

We're sent many different (and well-funded) messages about what's expected of us but are given few balanced viewpoints about our capabilities and strengths. We are beautiful or we're not beautiful, end of story.

The extreme end point of chasing the beauty ideal is, of course, death. According to the *New York Times* article by Larry Rohter in 2007, "In the Land of Bold Beauty, a Trusted Mirror Cracks," six Brazilian women tragically died of anorexia in a short span. The article traces the transformation of the Brazilian beauty ideal from the guitar-shaped frame (heavy on the waist, hips, and butt) to the Euro-American shrunken hourglass. Gisele Bundchen, the lanky Brazilian model, seems to epitomize this shift. Today, instead of wishing for larger bottoms (what Brazilian men have traditionally deemed attractive), Brazilian girls pine for the stick-thin figures popular in the rest of the industrialized world. Late model Ana Carolina Reston died in pursuit of the thin ideal, as did a handful of other Brazilian twenty-somethings. Mary del Priore, a historian quoted in the article, suggests, "Men are still resisting and clearly prefer the rounder, fleshier type. But women want to be free and powerful, and one way to reject submission is to adopt these international standards that have nothing to do with Brazilian society." While it's true these women may be bucking cultural tradition, it seems that now they're simply playing by a different set of rules, characterized by an alternative submission that proves lethal at times.[5]

Of course, skewed body image would take root in fashion and spread worldwide, but what about Olympic sports? One might think the Olympics would be the ultimate example of an arena where a woman's body, capable of running and lifting and throwing, would be considered a subject rather than an object. Sure enough, in 2012, more women competed in the London Olympics than in any other Olympic games in history. More American women made the US team than men, and they won their fair share of our nation's hefty gold medal count. By most appearances, a female athlete in London was prized for her strength, her endurance, her speed, and her skill. Bodies of different shapes and sizes were present, but we focused more on what these bodies were capable of doing, rather than how they looked, right?

Yes. Except for hearing about gold medalist gymnast Gabby Douglas's hair—occasionally at the expense of her gold medal accomplishments and the records she set for American women and women of color. Or weightlifter Holley Mangold's body weight—often at the expense of how much weight she was lifting. Or that news story reporting that the Brazilian women's soccer team was called "a bit heavy" by the coach of another team.[6]

Can we continue to move beyond these inconsequential details in our appreciation of female athleticism? Women can be strong and fit and powerful and fast and flexible and tough and determined and fierce, and the shape of their bodies is not as important as their prowess in sport. Our reporters and media people know this, of course, but they can't seem to stop measuring and reporting on women's femininity, even as they report on their achievements. The bias is so entrenched that it's almost invisible.

I was reminded of this bias when I took a community philosophy class. We addressed the topic *What are you?* Philosophically, there are three aspects to the self: body, mind, and heart. The professor asked us to comment on these variables. My classmates and I spoke about which elements we know for sure exist and which tend to dominate our lives. I commented that women seem to be more identified with their bodies than men; a greater part of our self-definition arises from our bodies.

As I provided sociobiological explanations for why a woman's appearance matters more, most women and some men agreed with me. I offered everything from evolutionary choices to the differential incidence of eating disorders by gender to prove my point. But a couple of men (including the instructor) were taken aback. They simply couldn't believe that now, in the twenty-first century, there was any gender difference in the way men and women identified with their bodies.

If you remember back to chapter 3, however, you'll recall that women don't speak of fat as an entity separate from ourselves: we speak of feeling fat or being fat. We *are* our bodies; many women think about them more than we think about anything else in our lives. Women may be dissatisfied with various elements in their lives (e.g., work, finances, relationships), but it's body dissatisfaction that packs the greatest punch. Men are appreciated for what they accomplish; women often find favor for how they appear. Men do. Women are. When we can't be what we think we're supposed to be, we turn that anger inward.

EXERCISE: From Object to Subject

Focus on what your body can do rather than how it looks. Make a list of twenty things your body is capable of doing. Are you able to swim or hang glide? Do you enjoy a loving hug? The more you focus on your body as subject rather than object, the better your body image will be.

What's Normal? Not Women

The title of this book is problematic for a lot of people. Some believe that by wondering if nearly every woman has a problem with food or weight, I'm conveying that something is wrong with our gender as a whole, that we have deviated from some norm of acceptability and now occupy a psychologically unhealthy space. In some ways, that's correct, but I hesitate to confer this truth because, at its heart, labeling women as deviant is about as unfeminist as you can get. Whenever I give an eating disorder diagnosis, I find myself wanting to highlight and interpret the myriad influences that result in an eating disorder as a way to prove that women aren't inherently abnormal, but that we are cultivated to be disordered by our culture—that wanting to eat less and wanting to *be* less prove that our society has been successful in brainwashing women and girls. Sometimes I think about diagnosing the culture, not the individual, and wonder if rather than diagnosing a woman with an eating disorder, we should be diagnosing her with living in the United States in the twenty-first century. Wrong time, wrong place.

The real truth is, all of psychiatry is subjective to some extent. What we define as a mental disorder, what symptoms we cluster under each disease, is largely a reflection of our cultural values and norms at that point in time. Right now in our culture, in terms of eating and food, we value willpower and control—thinness in a world of easy food availability. If you struggle with attaining this normal state, if you swing too far into restriction or use food in emotional ways or are too reactive to periods of deprivation, you may be labeled as having a disorder. Because the culture at large seems to see eating problems as problems of control, this diagnosis carries the connotation of "weak," therefore "less than." Women have been seen this way for centuries.

As social psychologist Carol Tavris writes in her book *The Mismeasure of Woman: Why Women Are Not the Better Sex, the Inferior Sex, or the Opposite Sex*, "In every domain of life, men are considered the normal human being, and women are 'ab-normal,' deficient because they are different from men."[7] This normal/abnormal dichotomy has been in existence for centuries. Traditionally, women are seen as the weaker sex, softer and less competent. In many cases, we're even seen as inherently diseased.

We can go as far back as the biblical telling of Adam and Eve to see this dynamic unfold. Eve, created out of a single rib of the fully intact Adam, is the one who falls prey to the serpent's trickery, eating the forbidden fruit and forever banishing the couple (and all of humanity) from the Garden of Eden.

On the more scientific side, Darwin posited that the males of every species are more highly evolved than the females due to the process of natural selection: they must attack their rivals while simultaneously charming their potential sexual partners. Males who are able to accomplish both tasks with success survive and reproduce, creating a population full of highly evolved males. Females, however, remain firmly entrenched in the evolutionary status quo. Men get stronger and better. Women don't; therefore, we're weaker, stunted.

This theory about males and females, formulated in the mid-1800s, helped inform classic Freudian theory, upon which a large chunk of current psychology is based. Freud's belief that women are the weaker sex led him and his contemporaries, in the 1890s, to diagnose women with a condition they called "hysteria," a word derived from the Greek word "hystera," meaning womb. (In ancient Greece, this condition was known as "wandering womb.") When women exhibited a loss of emotional control, their runaway uteri were to blame. Psychopathology was judged to be a problem with female anatomy, and just being a woman increased your susceptibility to mental illness. Conversion disorder (functional neurological symptom disorder), today's version of hysteria, is still diagnosed more commonly in women, but at least the disorder is no longer attributed to female anatomical dysfunction.[8]

That something is wrong with the female anatomy occupies another major tenet of Freudian theory. Do you ever look at your body in the mirror and notice that something's missing? Freudian theory suggests that once they realize that their genitals are different from their male counterparts', preschool-aged girls suffer from penis envy. In essence, we want what men have. More modern theorists argue that little girls might not covet the actual penis, but rather the power it connotes (power envy). Is it possible that women have learned that by chasing the beauty ideal, they can approximate the power of men? (Or at least experience power by association by attracting men with power?)

Even modern medical research, which is supposed to be as objective as possible, often agrees that the male body is right. Medical studies have traditionally been based on the norm of the "150-pound male." (Note that he's not just male, but also a certain weight—likely a weight that does not reflect our current growth trends.) This norm is meant to transfer to female populations. But when we test medications on male bodies and assume they will work the same way on female bodies, we're simply not doing good research.

Women and men are physiologically different, without a doubt, but are we really intrinsically prone to different emotional disorders and mental diseases? It's interesting to consider how psychiatric diagnoses are unabashedly misogynistic. More women are diagnosed as depressed, as eating disordered, as suffering from borderline, histrionic, and dependent personality disorders, and as struggling with certain classes of anxiety disorders, all raising the question of how normal is defined and why the female psychology—more openly emotional, more communicative, which in some way relate to many of the above diagnoses—is viewed as an unacceptable deviation from the norm. Carol Tavris comments on how women's status as the "second sex" à la Simone de Beauvoir, confers on us a host of psychological problems just by definition (and as evidenced by a trip down the self-help aisle in your local bookstore): "Women are irrational because of their hormones. They cry too much. They love too much. They talk too much. They are too dependent on unworthy men, but if they leave the men to fend for themselves, they are too independent, and if they stay with the men, they are codependent. They are too emotional, except when the emotion in question is anger, in which case they aren't emotional enough. They don't have correct orgasms, the correct way, with the correct frequency."[9]

Women, it seems, just can't get it right. Our natural emotions and behavioral proclivities are misunderstood. Even worse, they're pathologized. Women who feel otherized like this, who also exist in a cultural climate that values thinness above all else, may resort to disordered eating as a way to sidestep or cope with some of these cruel gender norms. They might still be "too emotional" or "not sexual enough," but at least they can try to get the body part right. And yet, by developing an eating disorder, they are made to seem even more abnormal.

We need to shift lenses and look at women independently from men. Why is it that women cry too much? Perhaps men don't cry enough. Every one of the problems discussed with women, as Tavris encourages us to imagine, could easily be flipped to diagnose a newfound problem with men. I'm not suggesting that we do this, but I am suggesting that we take a step back and stop condemning women for having emotions and being invested in relationships and for depending on others for connection and support. We need to stop diagnosing women for being women.

If we don't make a change soon, we may continue to be subjected to the daily message that all women are broken but can be fixed. And of course, this also translates to our bodies. As Naomi Wolf says in her classic book *The Beauty Myth: How Images of Beauty Are Used Against Women*, "Whatever is deeply, essentially female—the life in a woman's expression, the feel of her flesh, the shape of her breasts, the transformations after childbirth of her skin—is being reclassified as ugly, and ugliness as disease. . . . At least a third of a woman's life is marked with aging; about a third of her body is made of fat. Both symbols are being transformed into operable conditions—*so that* women will only feel healthy if we are two thirds of the women we could be."[10] We've been taught to believe there's *too much* of us, and that to be healthy, and therefore happy, we need to change who we are. I disagree. I think we need to change the discussion.

EXERCISE: Reverse Brainwashing

All of our negative beliefs about our bodies are socially constructed. When you find yourself having negative thoughts about your body, follow up each thought with the phrase *I've been brainwashed to think this way.*

I need to lose weight. I've been brainwashed to think this way.

I hate my arms. I've been brainwashed to think this way.

My face is too fat. I've been brainwashed to think this way.

If you get consistent with this afterthought, you'll start to think more critically about how culture has impacted your self-esteem, and you will chip away at some of the powerful brainwashing you've experienced.

Is Dieting Antifeminist?

Given all of the theories I've just presented, is it possible we're hurting ourselves, as women, by continuing to conform to the beauty ideal? I like this relatable quote by Kjerstin Gruys in her book about body image, *Mirror, Mirror Off the Wall: How I Learned to Love My Body by Not Looking at It for a Year*: "Could I still be a 'real' feminist if I shaved my legs and armpits? How about if I wore a push-up bra? Was I supremely naive to feel so empowered by a good hair day? And why did I feel so proud—as though I'd somehow 'made it'—when I was interviewed for a book titled *Sexy Feminism: A Girl's Guide to Love, Success, and Style*?"[11] In an effort to separate her self-worth from her appearance, Gruys goes a year without mirrors and soon finds out just how difficult it is to not think about her looks.

As women, we are socialized from birth to think about our beauty before our brains (as discussed in chapter 6). This is why it's so easy for us to slide into dieting and weight and shape obsessions. However, if it's wrong for society to believe the female body is faulty and in need of fixing, isn't it just as wrong for you as an individual to feel you need to drop a few pounds? Can you have it both ways? Can you be a feminist and want to lose weight?

Carmen is a 37-year-old woman who has wrestled with exactly this question.

> In college, I studied gender studies and began to identify with feminist thought. I was naturally someone who questioned the status quo, and I enjoyed learning about the social construction of gender and the campaign for women's rights. In law school, I studied gender law and policy. I identify as a feminist and, yes, I shave my legs. I look at my body and I often want to lose weight. Why? Because I've been indoctrinated by our culture. I get that. But part of being a feminist means that I can step back and realize what forces have contributed to the way that I think and then choose to act in a way that's most comfortable for me, which may sometimes be at odds with my political beliefs. Some may say that I'm acting in accordance with patriarchal values by shaving and wanting to lose a few pounds, but I'm still very much a feminist. I have to live in a society, and our society shames fat and glorifies thin. It reminds me of language.

> I'm Cuban-American and grew up speaking Spanish in
> my home. While Spanish is my first language, I have to
> speak English in America to get by. In the same way, it's
> easier to get by in our culture when you look the part. Is
> that antifeminist? Maybe it's just smart.

Some feminists and gender theorists believe that our cultural emphasis on female beauty is a tool designed to keep us from acquiring power or becoming more successful than men. Our fixation with thin may serve a similar purpose. There's something about a woman who eats daintily or a slight, frail-looking woman—she's less powerful and more malleable than her meatier counterparts.

All around us are images and plans and products and surgeries to help us get beautiful (and thin) and hold on to our youth. In *The Beauty Myth*, Naomi Wolf discusses this as "a violent backlash against feminism that uses images of female beauty as a political weapon against women's advancement: the beauty myth."[12] After all, if we're busy putting on makeup or going to the liposuction clinic, we won't have much time or energy left over for nation-building.

Wolf's backlash theory is persuasive, but others argue that women haven't crossed as many barriers as she suggests. Hall and Cohn, for instance, believe that disordered eating may actually result from women's unequal roles in the workplace. Despite key advances in workplace gender rights, the authors say, women continue to be underrepresented in high-power jobs, underpaid, and forced to work within a patriarchal structure that may be at direct odds with our inherent, feminine pull toward cooperation and interdependence. Even today, women earn 77 percent of what men do for performing the exact same job. We've tried to play the game, but we still have difficulty competing. And so, we resort back to a focus we know will get us far. We might not be able to control our promotions but surely we can control our physiques. We don't have gender privilege, but we can acquire thin privilege. Regardless of how far we've come, the authors go on to say, women are still being socialized to understand that beauty matters above all else. "How can a woman feel good about who she is on the inside if everyone else seems to focus on the outside?"[13] Author and feminist Julie Zeilinger believes that this hyperfocus on appearance stymies young female leaders. "By the time we're old enough to seriously consider becoming leaders, the majority of us are crippled by insecurities about the way we look, which we internalize and equate with our sense of worth on all levels."[14]

So, can you be a true feminist and still want to dip below your natural weight? Simply by refusing to accept our bodies as they are, are we all tacit supporters of the notion that to be successful, you must be thin? I'm reminded of a holiday weight-control tip that I found on the *Prevention* website and that appears on countless sites online. The tip states, "For the duration of the holidays, wear your snuggest clothes that don't allow much room for expansion."[15] When I first read this, I found myself cringing at the discomfort—physical and emotional—of constriction and the idea that expansion and growth are off the table. Is a diet just a modern-day corset?

If so, can we collectively work to throw diet and weight and shape obsessions, too, in the obsolete pile? Can we, armed with data and empowerment and will, recognize that these modern-day constraints are harmful, destructive, and just don't work? At least a corset could be removed at the end of the day. The emotional and physical impact of wanting to be smaller can have cascading consequences that last a lifetime. Let's limit these consequences by declaring weight fixation out of vogue.

Women versus Women: The Battle No One Wins

If we want to let go of our corsets, the first thing we need to do is face two truths: (1) we are often our own worst enemies, and (2) our second-worst enemies are other women. You know the "lookdown," right? The up-and-down stares women give each other when they meet, checking out each other's clothing, hair, makeup, accessories, and most important in the final review, bodies. Many of us probably do this unconsciously most of the day, every day. Author Pam Houston sums it up well: "I am walking down the street in Manhattan, Fifth Avenue in the lower Sixties, women with shopping bags on all sides. I realize with some horror that for the last fifteen blocks I have been counting how many women have better and how many women have worse figures than I do. Did I say fifteen blocks? I meant fifteen years."[16]

Women do this everywhere. I interviewed Leslie Goldman, author of *Locker Room Diaries*, to ask her about the female-female competition she observed during the time she spent researching women in her gym's locker room. Regarding the secret once-overs we give each other, she told me, "You can just see the thought bubble over their heads. 'Thank God she has a big butt,' or, 'Oh, she has cellulite,' or 'I wish my boobs were like this.' There's already enough competition and self-loathing. I think women should be joining together and supporting each other."[17]

Thirty-three-year-old Orly remembers one of the earliest triggers to her disordered eating just like it was yesterday:

> I had gone to one of those summer enrichment programs at a college up north before my senior year of high school. I quickly and happily fell in with the "cool" group of girls, and I was having tons of fun. One afternoon, we were at the lake, and another girl from our program walked by us, a girl around my size, wearing a bikini. "She should not be wearing that!" my friend commented. Instantly, I got really uncomfortable. I couldn't help but think that since I was about that size (and also wore a bikini that summer), that my friend was saying (or thinking) these unkind things about me. It was like this immediate shift. I decided to drastically cut back on what I was eating, and I began checking my body in front of the mirror multiple times a day, looking for any signs of weight loss. I guess you could call that the beginning of the end.

One of the ways we can support one another better is to simply refrain from commenting on one another's bodies. Avoid body talk of any kind—both criticisms and compliments—and find something else to talk about. If you see a woman being comfortable with her body, don't call her out on it—just let it go. As an example, I can point to a locker room experience I once had. When I stepped up to one of the vanity hairdryer stations, I let my towel slip from my chest to my waist. My neighbor caught my absent-minded action and said, "Must be nice to be comfortable enough to [insert let-it-all-hang-out gesture here]!" I suppose, but often it's function over form. Though I think this woman meant her evaluation as a compliment, I can only wonder at any negative thoughts she might have been thinking but wouldn't dare say, and I can't help but think that if I were a man in the men's locker room, the same behavior would go unnoticed. Women, as most of us know, are our worst critics.

Good, bad, positive, negative, can we just leave one another's bodies alone? When you see another woman, instead of instantly noticing and judging her hair, her clothing, her size, try this autocorrection: *I wonder what she was like as a little girl. I wonder what kind of music she likes, what her friends value most about her, what she dreams about, and what makes her happy.* Conceptualize her as a unique, whole individual rather than a combination of hair, clothing, and flesh.

Not too infrequently, female-female competition transcends the lookdown into actual aggression, as was occasionally witnessed on my blog. The fat versus the thin, the bingers versus the restrictors, me versus the adherent to whatever diet plan I was critiquing. The women on the blog were sometimes downright nasty, engaging in name-calling and hostility, losing sight of our common purpose. It saddened me to think that even when we were coming together to discuss a shared concern, sometimes we still had to tear each other apart.

Conclusion

As one of my blog readers noted,

> Ironically, the people most critical of women's bodies are typically other women! Have a little compassion, will ya? I realize, of course, that (many—not all!) women are so hard on themselves that they *must* be hard on others also. They cannot accept other women's imperfections, as it would mean, at least in part, accepting their own. Or so I see it. Anyway, maybe this all has some hidden good, as it's sparking a debate (not just on this blog, but nationwide, if not Western-world-wide), and maybe, just maybe more people will begin to see how ridiculous it is to devalue women for just being women.

I hope that she's right.

We need to shift radically the way we look at, talk about, and think about women's bodies. As women, we should lead the charge by starting out being kind to ourselves. We won't go far without a healthy measure of self-compassion. Perhaps then we'll be able to appreciate the divine beauty in one another without getting sidetracked with something so superficial as skin color, hair texture, or the size of one's hips. But we all need to get on board, each and every one of us. In the next chapter, you'll learn specific strategies designed to help you heal your relationships with food and your body. Rehearse them until they're committed to memory. Practice them daily. Spread the word. The only way we can challenge our nation's fixation with food and weight is to get smarter and louder and take a stand and fight back.

CHAPTER 8

⫻ Lose the Diet. Love Your Body. Eat in Peace.

*The need for change bulldozed a road
down the center of my mind.*
— MAYA ANGELOU

A CLASSIC JOKE IN THE PSYCHOLOGY FIELD asks, "How many psychologists does it take to change a light bulb?" The answer: "One, but the light bulb has to *want* to change." The same can be said with regard to disordered eating and poor body image. Do you want to change your relationship with food and your body? How fed up are you with constant food and body anxiety? How motivated are you to make these changes?

Up to this point, I have focused on describing the problem and offered theories as to its genesis. In this chapter, I offer you a solution to the status quo. Years ago, I developed an approach called Lose the Diet. Love Your Body. Eat in Peace. Here, you'll find ten practices that can help you achieve these goals. But first you need to ask yourself, Am I ready to change?

Preparing to Change

Before I present the ten practices, let's see if you're truly ready to make a change and improve your relationships with food and your body. Typically, when changing life behaviors, people pass through five stages:

1. Precontemplation. You have no intention of making a change, at least in the next six months or so. You may not even be aware that there's a problem.

2. Contemplation. You're planning on making a change sometime within the next six months. (Ready!)

3. Preparation. You're gearing up for change sometime within the next month. (Set!)

4. Action. You make the change. (Go!)

5. Maintenance. You continue to work on new behaviors and try to guard against relapse.[1]

Applying this process to your thoughts, feelings, and behaviors related to food and your body, ask yourself these questions:

- Are you thinking about addressing your food restriction, obsession, or compulsion?

- Would you like to return food to its natural role as sustenance and remove its powers to alternately calm you down and stir up your anxiety?

- Do you want to give up the idea of dieting?

- Are you fed up (no pun intended) with thinking uncontrollably about your weight and about food you'll eat or not eat?

- Are you tired of giving your energy to compulsive eating, exercising, weighing yourself, and generally despising your body and yourself?

- Are you willing to love yourself with 10, 20, or more extra pounds—and ready to accept your body the way it is right now?

If you said "yes" to at least one of the above questions, you're off to a good start. I'd like to move you along the stages of change to step three: preparing to take action. (Because really, what are you waiting for?)

In a body image workshop I led a number of years ago, a participant spoke about her self-hatred as a painful but necessary process. If she were to stop hating herself, she said, she'd let herself go and gain weight. In her case, self-hatred was a tool that she felt justified in using. When this self-hatred becomes too painful, when it keeps you from living in the moment, feeling secure in your relationships, enjoying food, finding joy in activities, or maybe even having any pleasure at all in your life, you might be ready to take action.

Letting go of behaviors you've been trained to see as virtuous can be scary. Though having an eating problem is not a comfortable way of being in the world, it is accepted by our society, and sometimes thinking about the perceived alternative—a loss of control, gaining weight, being viewed by others as undisciplined—can seem worse. Don't fool yourself. Holding on to disordered behavior is not making you a better person, a happier person, or even, necessarily, a thinner person. By continuing to put time and energy into hating yourself and your body, you are eroding your self-esteem. I want to teach you ways to build yourself back up so that your energy might be redirected into more productive parts of your life.

If you're still unsure about whether you're ready, start with an old-fashioned pros and cons list. List your disordered eating symptoms (e.g., extreme dieting, overeating, compulsive exercising, body checking, comparing yourself to images of celebrities) down the side of a page. Now create a column to list the pros. What are the benefits of having these behaviors? How do they help you? What do they help you feel (or not feel)? How do they improve your life? Do they positively impact your work, your relationships with family and friends, or your self-concept?

Now let's fill out the cons column. What is the cost associated with continuing these behaviors? Do they hurt you emotionally? Do they impact your family, your work, your social functioning, or your self-concept in a negative way?

Review the pros and cons. If the pros outweigh the cons, and if you feel you can continue as you are now, bookmark this page and come back to it in a few months. You may not be ready to change yet, but someday the balance may shift.

If you see significantly more costs than benefits associated with living the way you are now, if the cons outnumber or outweigh the pros, you may be ready to take the next step.

Ten Practices toward Lose the Diet. Love Your Body. Eat in Peace.

The practices below are what I've culled from fifteen years of research, counseling women, talking with groups, writing a blog, and as any intent scientist would do, practicing on myself. Some of them are so simple you can start today. Others will take more work, practice, and possible consultation with a professional who can guide you along. You may be surprised to note that most of the practices have nothing to do with food; instead, many are geared toward enriching your mind and well-being, a crucial step in helping you to move beyond your fixation on the physical.

Practice #1: Become an Intelligent Consumer

The media exposes you to a skewed version of the truth (see chapters 3, 4, and 5). Diets, they say, are effective weight-loss techniques. All it takes to achieve the ideal body is a little effort. Fat is responsible for all disease. Celebrities have naturally perfect bodies without the aid of restrictive diets, excessive exercising, or Photoshopping.

When you become an intelligent consumer, you learn that all of the above is untrue. You begin to question what you read, see, and hear. When you look at images of famous people or models, you ask, "Was she airbrushed?" You can't compare yourself to a celebrity because the playing field isn't fair. As supermodel Cindy Crawford reveals, "I always say even I don't wake up looking like Cindy Crawford."[2]

When you see endorsements of diet pills or plans, you wonder, *How much is this person being paid to say she's tried this and it works?*

When you're active on social media, you remember people are usually posting only the most flattering photos of themselves, taken in good lighting (and often with their hair and makeup done).

Most important, when you read scientific research, you pay attention to the influences that may have affected the facts you're being presented.

For example, who funded the study? Was it a drug company? A diet product? The results might not be as objective as you think. In *The Diet Myth: Why America's Obsession with Weight Is Hazardous to Your Health*, Paul Campos reports that many studies on obesity are conducted by physicians and weight-loss clinics intimately tied to the diet industry. By definition, this obfuscates the possibility of unbiased (read: ethical) research.[3]

Furthermore, many studies run multiple analyses of their data. This way, researchers can get creative and choose to publish the results that support their hypotheses and their products. Any amateur statistician can tell you that statistics are more an art than a science. If you look hard enough (and run enough analyses), you're bound to find something you hoped to see.

The informed consumer of scientific research should consider other factors, as well, when evaluating study claims:

- How many participants were in the study? (Generally, the more the better.) Was the sample diverse? Did the sample represent you? A study done on men, children, or mice might not apply to a grown woman.

- Were all data used, and if not, how can we explain why certain data were tossed?

- What types of statistical techniques were used?

- Were the participants and the researcher both aware of the experimental hypotheses? If so, that might influence (and artificially inflate) the results.

- How about that sneaky fellow, the placebo effect? Can the researchers really know without a doubt what brought about the results they recorded?

- What other factors might contribute to what seems like a causal relationship? Let's say you find a study that shows that people who eat kale every week are smarter than those who don't. Based on this study, does kale lead to greater intelligence? Not necessarily. It could also be that smarter people choose to eat kale.

- Where was the research published? Peer-review journals are best. Even research that's remarkably poor can be published in a substandard publication for a fee.

All kinds of factors need to be considered when evaluating weight-loss research. Unfortunately, the scientific value of studies is often obscured by the emotionality, funds, and media involved. Reading, and consequently citing, a study at face value is often not enough. By questioning scientific research using the list above, you will think like an entry-level researcher and become a wiser consumer who isn't as easily duped by the latest craze.

Lastly, being an intelligent consumer means developing an awareness of how you're influenced by various media. Gone are the days when we'd have to open a magazine or turn on the television to fall prey to advertising. Now we find advertisements online, in our e-mail inboxes, on our Facebook pages, on our Internet radios—everywhere we turn.

An article in 2007 cited market research estimating that the average US resident was exposed to approximately five thousand advertising messages a day.[4] Can you imagine if this study were conducted now? You're constantly being sold a product, an image, a dream. Weight-loss companies will go to extreme measures to force you to fork over your dollars, including misrepresenting data, distorting images, and making false promises.

Remember, no single product, plan, or program can reliably result in long-term weight loss—only an unhealthy game of weight cycling. Don't be fooled.

Practice #2: Return to Intuitive Eating

I hope by now you understand that diets don't work. If you truly want to make peace with food, it is important that you fully commit never to diet again.

Even if a new and improved plan surfaces on the market.

Even if your typical eating pattern gets derailed.

Even, and especially if, you happen to gain some weight. Going back to dieting is revisiting part of what caused the problem in the first place.

Just as important as giving up dieting is abolishing the plethora of food rules you may have created over the years. Do you have certain rules about when to eat, what to eat, or how much to eat? Do these rules dominate over your bodily signals, cravings, and common sense? If you ever want to eat in peace, then you'll have to do away with these rules, too.

Instead I want you to try intuitive eating, as explained by Evelyn Tribole and Elyse Resch in their book of the same name.[5] Intuitive eating quite simply involves eating when you're hungry and stopping when you're full. It also involves, in general, eating what you want when you want. For chronic dieters, or most anyone who has spent a lifetime labeling foods as "good" or "bad," the notion of having what you want when you want sounds absurd. You'll lose control completely and end up gaining weight—that's the ultimate fear.

However, you might be surprised to learn that intuitive eating, practiced according to the guidelines below, will help you establish a healthier relationship with food, one that will free you of the constant thoughts about what you should or shouldn't eat. Eating intuitively will put food back in its proper place in your life—as sustenance and as pleasure, but not as something that controls you, dictates your mood, and has so much power that your life revolves around it. The goal here is not to eat recklessly, but rather to limit your experience of emotional eating and, if you're above your natural weight because of overeating, to possibly help you to return to your natural weight.

Here's how intuitive eating works, demonstrated by an experiment I conducted on myself. Years ago, I had baked a couple of carrot cakes, trying to perfect my recipe in time for a friend's approaching birthday. The cream cheese–frosted remains sat atop my kitchen counter, flirting with me across the room with that sexy come-hither aroma. One morning, I decided I wanted to eat that carrot cake.

Carrot cake for breakfast? That's illegal! my inner voice advised.

Since I was testing out intuitive eating, however, I forged ahead and enjoyed the perfect slice.

Later, when I was hungry for another meal, I again craved carrot cake, so I had another slice. And so the story went for several other meals. A couple of days later, I tired of carrot cake and reintegrated other foods.

Intuitive eating involves trusting your physiology. Your body will not always crave foods that are high in sugar and fat and salt. If you don't believe me, all I can do is ask you to repeat my carrot cake experiment and let me know your results. While you may crave certain foods to start, eventually your body will take over and force you to choose what you need to nourish it correctly.

Intuitive eating also involves choosing foods not just based on how they taste but how they fuel your body and make you feel. Have you ever noticed that you have more energy after a bowl of oatmeal than a doughnut? If you eat intuitively, you're going to consider this information when you make your food choices.

Eat what your body craves when you're hungry; stop when you're full. We were born knowing how to do this instinctively, but somewhere along the way we got the notion that we need to eat three meals a day, no snacking. Intuitive eating means getting rid of these rules from the outside world and simply listening to your body.

Where do you even start? Begin by becoming acquainted with your hunger and satiety cues. You should, at any given point, be able to rate your own hunger. I like to use this scale:

0	Empty (physically faint, very cranky)
1	Ravenous
2	Very hungry
3	Hungry
4	Slightly hungry
5	Neutral
6	Pleasantly satisfied
7	Full
8	Very full
9	Stuffed/bloated
10	Nauseous/ill

Where are you right now? Where were you before your last meal? After? I urge intuitive eaters to try to stay (all day!) between a 3 and a 7. If you dip below a 3, eat a snack. If you've rounded 7, stop eating. (Note: For those in the thick of anorexia nervosa, hunger/satiety cues can be distorted, so they might not be reliable as indicators here.)

How often should you eat according to this strategy? Most people do best with three meals and one to three snacks a day. Try not to go more than a few hours without food. Use your hunger as a guide. When you get hungry, eat. Not eating when you're hungry doesn't mean you win. There is no prize.

What I described above covers the physical aspects of intuitive eating. However, you must also reframe your cognitive and emotional responses to hunger and satiety. What is your first thought following a hunger pang? Does it sound like one of these?

- *I can't be hungry—I just ate.*

- *I shouldn't have any more calories today.*

- *Ugh!*

How about your first feeling?

- Worry

- Anger

- Despair

I want you to practice perceiving your hunger differently. Experiment with celebrating hunger, and remember, it's not a flaw. Hunger is your body working as it was designed to do. Reframe your responses the next time you feel a hunger pang, and try substituting a different thought:

- *I may have eaten recently, but I guess I could use something else.*

- *Rather than counting calories, I'm going to try to attend to my body's signals and have that be my eating guide.*

- *Woo-hoo!*

With hunger as your guide, you might eat more frequently throughout the day. You might also begin to eat less on each occasion. With each "woo-hoo" experience, you're learning to respect your hunger, which teaches you, among other things, how to respect your fullness and satiety.

Responding to hunger in this manner means being present in the current moment and responding to your bodily cues. It means transcending the shoulds of food (e.g., "I shouldn't eat now; I shouldn't eat this much") to focus on the messages your body is providing. Responding to hunger in the moment highlights experience over rigidly held beliefs and is therefore more flexible, adaptable, and ultimately more psychologically healthy.

Just like hunger, your experience of fullness, too, requires a paradigm shift. Can you begin to celebrate fullness as your body's way of letting you know that you fed it adequately, that you are providing it with proper nutrition? Fullness is your body's way of saying, "Enough for now." Know that when you eat intuitively, you'll eat again as soon as your body gives you the signal to do so. Fullness, particularly for women who struggle with emotional or compulsive eating, may signal sadness, as our bodies are giving us a sign to stop when our minds might be interested in something else. Ever think about your first thought as you get full from eating?

- *Oh, no, I ate too much! I'm going to gain weight.*
- *No! I don't want to stop! This tastes too good.*
- *When do I get to eat again?*

How about your first feeling?

- Worry
- Anger
- Despair

Practice replacing these thoughts with new ones:

- *Great, I fed my body what it needed.*
- *My body is saying it's time to stop.*
- *It doesn't matter how much food is left on my plate; my body is saying enough for now.*
- *This food tastes good, and I'd like to continue eating it, but if I do, I'll be stuffed and won't feel good after.*
- *I'll come back for more when I'm hungry again.*

And what about satisfaction? Many who have dysfunctional relationships with food experience fullness but rarely feel satisfied because they are so restrictive with what types of food they eat. Their bellies might be full, but their minds are still craving what they didn't allow themselves to have. Can you experiment with aiming for fullness and satisfaction when you eat? Many who avoid eating satisfying foods end up overeating, either now or later. Have you ever had the experience of eating much more than you needed because you didn't get what you wanted? Some have described to me the experience of standing in the kitchen and picking at foods they didn't really want because they were too tired to make (or get) what they really craved.

Others discuss trying so hard to be good, perhaps avoiding sweets, only to cave later in the day because the original craving just won't subside. Instead, aim for fullness with a healthy dose of satisfaction.

If you have a tendency to eat compulsively, remember, you are likely not addicted to food but rather the diet-binge cycle. Authors Jane Hirschmann and Carol Munter, in their book *Overcoming Overeating: How to Break the Diet/Binge Cycle and Live a Healthier, More Satisfying Life*, equate compulsive eating with a healthy rebellion against diets.[6] By learning to respect what your body wants, you can quell that rebellion and keep it under control. Their approach allows you to eat whatever you're craving in a given moment and focuses on equalizing different kinds of food, so that you can arrive at a place where a carrot has the same value as a slice of carrot cake. Whenever you're hungry, you're encouraged to ask yourself what you're craving: Are you in the mood for something sweet? Salty? Crunchy? Mushy? Hot? Cold? Time and time again, Hirschmann and Munter have found that people may make some nonnutritious choices early on, but eventually their bodies regulate and they begin to crave, at different times, foods across the spectrum.

This approach, or aspects of it, may seem radical to you, particularly in a culture that preaches regular meals, precision, restriction, monitoring, and self-loathing. It might not work for everyone, but I've found that it can be quite helpful for women who have historically cycled through the diet-binge chain. If you'd like to disempower the hold that food has on you, experiment with these tips. You may be surprised at how much they change your life.

Practice #3: Fully Nurture Yourself

There is more to you than a nourished and healthy body. Are you living a nourished life? Is your world enriched by meaningful relationships and connections, professional purpose, and spiritual awareness? Do you regularly engage in hobbies, interests, and other passions?

On a scale of 1 to 10, where 1 is "Not at all fulfilled" and 10 is "Extremely fulfilled," how would you rate your fulfillment in the following areas?

Relationships:
  with family members
  with friends
  with your partner, if you have one (or with the people you date)
  with your children, if you have them
  with yourself
Professional life
Community involvement
Spirituality
Finances
Interests or hobbies

For those areas of life in which you are lacking fulfillment, what can you do to beef up your nourishment? Can you focus on nurturing your relationships? Joining a group or club? Donating your time to a cause? These are all behaviors that can yield greater fulfillment and may, over time, result in less of a focus on food and shape.

Practice #4: Practice Self-Compassion
You can take some steps toward recovery even before you change your eating or address how you feel about your body. Self-compassion is one of them. How do you speak to yourself?

Do you operate out of self-love or self-abuse? I'd argue that you cannot make a change beginning from a place of self-abuse. The self-loving part of you will always step in and sabotage your plan (as well it should!).

Right now, a big push in psychology (including in the work with eating disorders) is the concept of self-care. How do you comfort, soothe, and show kindness to yourself? Are you compassionate, gentle, and patient, or are you harsh, punitive, and unyielding? What language do you use with yourself? Is it angry, hurtful, and condemning?

So much behavior, particularly related to eating and our bodies, is motivated either by self-care or self-abuse. Eating when you're hungry? Self-care. Exercising when you're tired or sick or because you have to get rid of the fat? Self-abuse. Allowing yourself to have a food you crave? Self-care. Eating when you're stuffed? Self-abuse.

Refusing to eat certain items, to bring certain food items into your home (especially those you crave) or to have just a couple of cookies (because that would mean you wouldn't stop) communicates, "I don't trust myself." Exercising to the point of discomfort, pushing yourself when you're tired, sick, or just don't want to communicates, "I deserve to be uncomfortable and to be punished."

I know that access to certain foods can lead to overeating, but that just raises the need to address why the overeating is happening. Yes, sometimes exercise can be enjoyable or lift your mood when you're down, but it's not fun when you're tired or weak or pushing yourself beyond what your body is willing to give.

Think about what you're saying to yourself when you make decisions that feel like deprivations or corrections. *I don't deserve what I want. I can't trust myself. I need to be punished.* If you repeat these over and over, your self-esteem doesn't stand a chance.

Karen Horney, a pioneering psychoanalyst who followed in the footsteps of Freud, spoke of the "Tyranny of the Should," the self-haunting that occurs when we compare how we are to how we think we should be.[7] Focusing on this discrepancy results, as you'd expect, in significant distress. The solution, according to psychologists, is to avoid the use of "should"—not just to remove the word from our vocabulary but to be more compassionate with ourselves and lighten up our often unrealistic expectations. The next time you have one of the following "should" thoughts, beep yourself, and try to reframe the thought:

I should exercise for an hour today. (I might choose to exercise for an hour today if that feels right for my body.)

I shouldn't eat that doughnut. (I'd like to eat that doughnut, or I get a sugar crash after I eat a doughnut, so I'm going to choose not to have that now.)

I should get the salad. (I prefer to get the salad.)

I should stick to my diet at all costs. (There are two problematic words in this sentence: "should" and "diet.")

Beware also the relatives of "should": "have to," "need to," "want to" (with sufficient angst). Why are these words so damaging? They set you up for unrealistic expectations. The truth is, it's sometimes challenging to exercise consistently, avoiding pleasurable foods can rob you of satisfaction, and it's difficult to shrink your body below its natural weight. When you get caught up in the "should" (instead of the "could" or the "would like to"), you set yourself up for disappointment and self-reproach, both of which play an integral role in sabotaging your personal goals and unsteadying an already shaky self-regard.

Instead of issuing "should" statements to yourself, I'd like you to take another approach: Can you forgive yourself for being imperfect? For making mistakes each day? For not getting it right? For failing to meet your expectations each and every time? For just getting by when you wanted to excel? For walking when you wanted to run? For eating more than you'd like? For weighing more than you'd like? Even for engaging in unhealthy measures to control how you look?

Those who struggle with eating problems often have significant difficulty with self-forgiveness. But consider the costs of not forgiving, criticizing, punishing, and self-attacking. This stance is likely to create more of the original transgressions. I work with a large percentage of my clients on practicing imperfection. For most of us, this is a life skill that must be learned. Being imperfect may challenge many of your preconceived ideas. Practice and you will get better at it. When you make a mistake, reframe this as an opportunity for you to get more comfortable with imperfection.

If you work on this one practice alone, you'll be a happier, more content person. In the words of Ralph Waldo Emerson, "Finish each day and be done with it. You have done what you could. Some blunders and absurdities no doubt crept in; forget them as soon as you can. Tomorrow is a new day; begin it well and serenely and with too high a spirit to be encumbered with your old nonsense."[8]

Practice #5: Explore and Create Personal Values
Aside from what you eat and how much you weigh, what is important to you in life? What are your priorities? Exploring these questions can be an important guide in the recovery process. Do you value ambition or achievement? Independence? Financial security? Friendships? Family and

parenting? Fun? Spirituality or religion? Giving back to the community? Learning new things? Inner peace?

Once you uncover what you value, your next task is to see if you are setting goals consistent with your values. Goals are concrete statements about what you would like to achieve. For example, you may value work and ambition and choose to set goals around this value (e.g., "I will reach out to several business contacts each week").

You can also explore whether or not your behavior is consistent with your values. Are you acting as if family or friendships or community are important to you? How do you spend your free time? How do you spend your free thought? Often, women with disordered eating spend a significant amount of time thinking about food and their bodies, eating (or not eating), or somehow trying to manipulate their bodies into smaller, thinner shapes. Usually, many of these thoughts and behaviors are inconsistent with their core values. Recognizing this discrepancy can help you refocus your efforts and energies on what is really meaningful to you. According to the developers of Acceptance and Commitment Based Therapy, who highlight the importance of values in therapy, you'll know you're operating out of your values when you experience "intense vitality, contact, presence, or purpose."[9] It just doesn't happen the same way with a focus on food, weight, or shape.

Practice #6: Re-create Exercise

Do you remember what it felt like to run around the playground during grade-school recess? To soar through the air on the monkey bars? To ride bikes down back roads with friends? To choreograph a dance with your sister? To splash around the pool? Do you remember how much fun movement used to be?

It's not until we age and want to lose or maintain weight that we begin to call all of this fun "exercise" and start to think of activity using a negative, punitive tone. "Fun" is something we want to do; "exercise" becomes something we should do. Redefining exercise means re-creating your original (recreational) relationship with physical activity—making it fun again. I encourage you to think about what you enjoy and find activities that don't feel like a chore. Acknowledge that you are designed to move and that exercise causes all kinds of feel-good chemicals to swirl around in your brain and body. Understand that exercise results in reduced anxiety and depression and improved self-esteem. Accept the fact that the more active you are, the healthier your body is.

Exercise is a wonderful thing. Unfortunately, that's not the case for most people I know. It seems I'm usually either working with people to begin an exercise program or, on the other extreme, to back off of an exercise regime they don't enjoy but feel compelled to do. As a psychologist who specializes in eating and body issues, who also has a master's degree in exercise and sport science and has been certified as a personal trainer for almost twenty years, I am uniquely positioned to comment on both sides of the exercise spectrum, from underexercise to compulsive exercise. We know that about 50 percent of people who begin an exercise program will drop out, often the

HOW TO DEVELOP A HEALTHY RELATIONSHIP WITH EXERCISE

1. Cross-train. Trainers have been talking for eons about the physiological benefits of cross-training, but cross-training has significant mental benefits, too. Participating in different activities throughout the week (month or year) reduces emotional burnout.

2. Get outside. There's something about fresh air and the sights, smells, and sounds of city or country living that can contribute to the psychological benefits of fitness. Nature, too, is a natural mood booster. True, some may also enjoy the sights (maybe not the smells) of their local gym, but still, I recommend that, weather permitting, you mix it up a bit.

3. Ban the gym. Speaking of the gym, consider your relationship with your local workout facility. If you hate going there, it's going to be an uphill battle all the way, and chances are, you'll drop out. If the gym connotes discomfort or punishment, choose another venue you actually look forward to visiting. Play tennis. Go hiking. Take salsa lessons. There is absolutely no need to go to the gym if that's not your thing. Adrenaline junkie? Try rock climbing, ocean swimming, mountain biking. You'd be impressed at how infinitely more thrilling chasing the speed limit while cycling downhill can be versus parking yourself on the stationary bike at the gym.

first six months.[10] Why? Because they don't like what they're doing. Because they burn out. Because life gets in the way. If you follow the tips in, "How to Develop a Healthy Relationship with Exercise," you'll be more likely to commit to healthy activity over the long haul because you'll actually enjoy what you're doing. Remember, the goal is to choose an exercise lifestyle that will work for the rest of your years.

I think it's important to emphasize here that you're more likely to persist if you conceptualize exercise as something you choose to do for your physical and mental health, or because it's fun, rather than something you must do to burn calories or control your weight. In my mind, this reframe is critical toward enhancing exercise adherence. If you don't love what you're doing, you are more likely to leave your routine lying in the dust when you don't see immediate weight-loss results. Be sure, too, to find fitness instructors who

4. Get your soundtrack on. Studies show that we'll work out longer and harder when accompanied by good music. I love my music collection so much that I look forward to the movement it commands. You, too, can create a personal dance party on your MP3 player. For more of a challenge, choose faster-paced music, as we unconsciously move our bodies to the beat.

5. Set goals. It's incredibly motivating to have a project or a goal to work toward. Sign up for your first 5K (or muddy buddy race, if that's your thing). Join a summer basketball league, knowing that you'd like to be in fighting shape before the league begins. Having some sort of goal or deadline can enhance your fitness commitment and keep you on track.

6. Forget the weight. Exercise because it feels good and contributes to physical and psychological health, not because it burns calories or helps you lose or maintain weight. Those who begin exercise programs to lose weight often drop out when they don't see the immediate desired results. On the other extreme, exercise can become disordered as individuals seek to burn off each additional calorie they've consumed. Exercise is a privilege, not a punishment for consumption. I wish that all group fitness instructors would, in their prompts during class, focus on strength, health, and fun rather

than calories and weight. More than fifteen years ago, I wrote my master's thesis on the mood-enhancing properties of exercise, and I still stand behind that research. Exercise results in reduced depression and anxiety and increased self-esteem. Work out with these benefits in mind.

7. Be consistent. Hemming and hawing about whether or not to work out today creates too much room for bailing. Have a set schedule that you commit to, unless you are sick or something urgent arises. Consider fitness to be a part of your everyday routine.

8. Take it easy. Yes, it is possible to be consistent and to take it easy. Schedule days off. This one is particularly challenging for those who have a compulsive relationship with exercise, but for that reason alone, it's important to achieve. The body (and the mind) need some time to recover. Taking a couple of days off per week allows you to come back clearer, stronger, and more determined. Schedule weeks off here or there throughout the year to recover more fully and further increase your drive. Prove that you have a healthy relationship with exercise by taking time off for work and family obligations, travel, illness, and surgeries without suffering guilt, anxiety, or irritability.

9. Embrace the grays. Taking it easy also involves reducing the black-and-white, all-or-nothing thinking and behavior around exercise and instead embracing the grays: Despite what almost everyone I work with believes, I still espouse that fifteen minutes of exercise is better than nothing. If you don't have the time or energy to put in a full workout, do what you can. Trust me, it still counts. On a related note, your workout should not feel like forty-five minutes of physical torture. Many people dislike exercise because they equate it with pain. Back off to a degree where you feel challenged but not distressed, especially if you're having an off day. Give yourself permission to dial back the effort. Your run can turn into a walk, your kickboxing class into a yoga class across the gym. And yes, it still counts.

10. Practice gratitude. Take a moment to remember how lucky you are to choose to move your body. Be thankful for functioning limbs, a healthy heart and lungs, and the lifestyle wherewithal that allows you to have the time, space, and energy to move.

emphasize the health-enhancing properties of exercise. You are working out for pleasure and fitness, not as penance. Cookies and cake are not bad. You do not need to atone for eating them. Exercise (with or without cookies or cake) is beneficial to your physical and psychological health.

Practice #7: Find Meaning and Purpose beyond Yourself

Can getting in touch with your greater purpose, or at least being open to the idea that there has to be more than this, help you recover from an eating issue? I think it can. I'm not talking about religion per se (unless this suits you), but rather a sense of what your purpose is here on earth. For some, the purpose is to be a good person and to live a good life. Others might believe they are here to learn a valuable lesson. Those who are less spiritually inclined might think that they are here simply to continue the species.

For many with eating disorders, life becomes so constricted (and restricted) that their purpose becomes eating less or weighing less. I don't know what your purpose here is, but I do know it can't be to restrict, maintain a certain weight, or hate your body. You have more to offer than that.

In my practice, I often ask women how they want to look back on their lives as they approach the end. I'll ask you the same. Looking back on your life, what do you want to say you were? What do you want to say you did? How do you want others to remember you? Of all the times I've asked these questions, not one woman has answered that nearing death, she wants to look back over her life and be sure that she was thin.

The irony is, we spend almost the entirety of our lives chasing a goal that we acknowledge doesn't matter one bit at the end. If it doesn't matter then, it shouldn't matter now.

Practice #8: Channel Your Inner Buddha

A number of concepts culled from Buddhism (or Eastern philosophies as a whole) have proven to be integral to recovery from disordered eating. Even if you practice another religion, these concepts may appeal to you because they are more about shifting your mental perspective than who or what you worship. Dialectical behavior therapy (DBT), a type of cognitive behavior therapy, has adapted a number of Buddhist concepts in its approach. Three that I find particularly useful are mindfulness, nonjudgmental acceptance, and gratitude.

Mindfulness

What is mindfulness? In *Full Catastrophe Living: Using the Wisdom of Your Body and Mind to Face Stress, Pain, and Illness*, Jon Kabat-Zinn defines it as attending to your experience in the moment.[11] Mindfulness involves simply being aware of your experience, not evaluating or judging what occurs.

How often do you practice mindfulness—being fully present? When you're out in the world, are you focused on the sights and sounds around you, or are you instead concentrating on how your belly juts out in the reflection of a store window?

How often do you eat mindfully? When you eat, are you paying attention to taste, color, heat, texture, hunger, and fullness, or are you zoned out, paying attention to what you should or shouldn't be eating, focusing on those around you, the media, what happened a few hours ago, or what might happen next?

I once attended a mindful eating exercise at a destination spa. Before we chose our food from a buffet, we were instructed not to focus on the shoulds of eating, but rather on what appealed to us. I piled food on my plate, paying attention to vibrant color and texture. I stood over a bowl for a moment, thinking, *I should probably add some flax seed*, but quickly caught myself and headed back to the table to begin the exercise.

For ten minutes, we were to eat mindfully—to meditate over our food, with awareness and without conversation. That ten minutes felt like an eternity.

Have you ever timed how long it takes you to eat breakfast, especially if you're not talking to someone else, watching TV, reading the paper, or otherwise multitasking? I'm guessing most of us, myself included, scarf down our food in fewer than ten minutes, and usually with one or more distractions.

By staring at my plate for ten minutes, I learned how to pay attention to my appetite, as well as color, texture, taste, and even sound. (It turns out I loved both the texture of oatmeal and the squishy sound it makes when it's stirred.) I learned that some foods I previously ate for my health, like omelettes and raspberries, I didn't even like, while others, like strawberries, were beautiful in ways I hadn't previously noticed. I also noticed for the first time that ten minutes at a table with several other women is a really long time to go without speaking. The enforced silence made me realize how conditioned we are to communicate at mealtimes, to focus on others (and other things) rather than what we're ingesting. Without these distractions, I easily registered my satiety, putting my fork down at the first sign of fullness.

I encourage you to try the same experiment the next time you're at a buffet or potluck dinner. Can you select what you really want and take mental notes about your choices?

You can also make a change at home by thinking about what kind of environment or context you create for dining. A 2012 study out of Cornell University found that diners who ate in ambience-enriched Hardee's restaurants (think mood lighting, music, and tablecloths) ate significantly less and reported more enjoyment of their food than their counterparts dining in the typical Hardee's interior. Maybe we don't have the time, energy, or wherewithal to create the perfect dining experience for each meal, but can we use this data to improve our surroundings as best we can?[12]

Nonjudgmental Acceptance

Nonjudgmental acceptance means being open to what happens, not what we want to have happen. It means throwing evaluations (negative and positive) out the window and working toward accepting what we experience and who we are.

Ask yourself: How often do you find yourself casting judgments, toward others, yourself, or life in general? Are you accepting of your body the way it is right now? When you don't accept your body, but rather stand in judgment of the many imperfections you perceive, what kind of message do you think that sends you? Do you think that mind-set makes it easier or more challenging to accomplish your goals?

Practice not judging. To start, look around the room you're in and observe what you see. Just observe and describe. "The couch is gray" and "The lights are on" are observations. "The carpet looks bad" or "I like that picture" are judgments. See if you can look around for an entire minute (it's longer than you think) without casting any judgments at all. Now, imagine spending that judgment-free minute looking down at your naked self!

Gratitude

Gratitude is a concept commonly discussed in spiritual practices. Practicing gratitude is straightforward: focus on what you have rather than what you don't. The goal is to take stock of your blessings rather than what you see lacking.

Have you ever noticed that it's virtually impossible to practice gratitude and hate your body at the same time? What is it that you have (versus have not) in your life? Can you highlight areas of abundance rather than deprivation? Sure, you may not have been blessed with model height, but your legs are healthy and allow you to walk.

This shift in mind-set can be profitable across the board. Some research shows that a deprivation mind-set (even when the deprivation isn't about food) can increase the likelihood of our eating higher-calorie foods.[13] Each day, take time to focus on what is going well in your life. Some days, this exercise may feel like a stretch (e.g., "At least I have a bed to sleep in"), but it's important to do. Be grateful for what you have and increase your opportunities for gratitude. Where can you add indulgences that don't cost much? Can you treat your senses with appealing scents, comfortable fabrics, enticing flavors, soothing visuals, and melodic sounds? Doing so can ease distress, increase our experience of pleasure, and, perhaps most important, communicate to ourselves that we are worth it.

Practice #9: Create a Body-Positive Environment

For many women, loving your body is one of the hardest practices there is. In fact, most people who are working on their relationships with food and their bodies report that they are able to make changes in how they eat long before they are able to improve their body image. Coming to grips with your shape and size can seem monumental, and in a culture that seems predicated upon body hatred, this practice often feels like running into the wind.

Can you act *as if* you love your body, even if you're not quite there? Try these tips to start:

- Refrain from attacking your body with verbal and visual assaults.

- Take care of your body, providing it with adequate nutrition, sleep, medical attention, and other self-care behaviors.

- Exercise for health and enjoyment, not for punishment or compensation.

- Wear clothing that fits, is comfortable, and flatters your physique.

- Participate in activities that you enjoy, without letting your size keep you sidelined or from enjoying these activities.

- Maintain a healthy sexual and romantic life (your body image isn't an obstacle to your sexuality).

- Treat your body well, and if finances allow, go for massages, pedicures, and so on.

- Accept that while you might prefer to be thinner, taller, tanner, or more toned, this is your body now.

For now, you may choose to view body love as aspirational; don't expect to get there immediately, but aim to get there someday. A few steps (like those above) can help you toward this goal. The first step (especially important) involves working to reduce or eliminate your body hatred. Do you consistently think body-negative thoughts? Do you behave in a way that disrespects your body? Many women I see in my practice speak to and treat themselves in a downright abusive fashion. Bringing your awareness to these behaviors can be a powerful intervention.

Remember that sage advice from Bambi's friend Thumper, "If you can't say something nice, don't say nothing at all"? With regard to how we speak to ourselves about our bodies, this advice is spot-on. Observe your internal body talk. Acknowledge your negative thoughts, all the judgments and criticisms, and work toward eliminating them. In the beginning, you may not be able to replace the negative thoughts with loving thoughts, but you may be able to gently challenge the clatter. Try distracting yourself and moving on to something else. Pick up a book. Go for a walk. Call a friend. Spending time criticizing your body is a useless endeavor.

If you're ready for the next step, try an exercise designed to help you accept your body. Thomas Cash, in *The Body Image Workbook: An 8-Step Program for*

Learning to Like Your Looks, describes the process of mirror desensitization.[14] Psychologists will often encourage patients with phobias to expose themselves to their fears with the idea that with time and exposure, their anxiety will fade. Frightened of spiders? Hang out with one for an hour. Scared of elevators, heights, subways, crowds, or rats? Come to New York City!

With mirror desensitization, try to create a "Ladder of Body Areas," in which you rank your body parts on a satisfaction hierarchy. The part or parts of your body that you're most satisfied with go on the bottom, while those you detest the most go up top. For example, maybe your hair and eyes are at the bottom of the list and your stomach is at the top. Once you've created your ladder, you're ready to face the mirror.

Stand in front of it and begin by looking at a particular body part that doesn't cause you much distress to view—maybe even a part of your body you like. Breathe. Relax. Think pleasant thoughts. If you can do this calmly, then you're ready for the next step.

According to Cash, move on to a body part that causes a bit more discomfort for you. Look at this body part for a full minute. Shut your eyes and relax. Cash encourages you to systematically work your way up your "Ladder of Body Areas" until you reach the top—the part of your body you find most difficult to view. Does this happen immediately? Of course not. Mirror desensitization will usually take multiple sessions. Try a couple of body parts at a time. If you can't relax, breathe, and avoid judgment, stay at that particular rung until you can.

Is this hard work? Potentially. Impossible? Not at all. The goal is to work your way toward what I call "mirror indifference." When you become mirror indifferent, you can look or not; it doesn't matter. You don't feel the need to pause at every mirror you see, nor do you avoid mirrors because they cause you pain. Your reflection says nothing about who you are. A mirror, is, after all, just a piece of broken glass.

When you're ready, I also advise you to do away with your scale. Some find it difficult to toss their scales cold turkey. You can start with baby steps. If you're weighing yourself more than once a day, cut it down to once daily over a period of time. Eventually drop down to once a week, then once a month. Anticipate that you may experience anxiety as you reduce your scale time.

That's normal, and it will decrease with time. Now would be the perfect time to schedule something fun as a reward for not weighing. Be careful of other behaviors creeping up as compensation. If you have a tendency to stare at different parts of your body, or even grab or touch them to check them, you'll want to target these, too. The same goes for using different-sized clothing from your wardrobe as a metric. That dress that fit ten years ago that every so often you try on with the hopes of getting the zipper up? Toss it. If you find yourself engaging in any of these behaviors, just note what you're doing and redirect your attention elsewhere. Notice, redirect, repeat if necessary.

Lastly, when the mirror, the scale, and your subjective assessments cease to have a hold on you and you find yourself issuing fewer (or maybe no) judgmental comments to yourself or your reflection, consider breaking up with your eating and body image problems.

In *Life Without Ed*, eating disorder sufferer Jenni Schaefer crafts a declaration of independence from her disorder, which she calls Ed:

> Jenni, therefore, solemnly publishes and declares that
> she is free and independent; that she is absolved from
> all allegiance to Ed, that all connection between Ed
> and her ought to be totally dissolved, and that as a free
> and independent woman she has the full power to eat,
> live in peace, and to do all other acts and things which
> independent people do.[15]

She prefers a legalese approach, but I like a good old-fashioned break-up letter. If you've ever broken up with someone via letter, e-mail, or text, you know how it works. Now's your chance to break up with your eating problem.

What goes in the letter is your choice, but I recommend the following template.

> Dear [scale, mirror, calorie-counting conscience, etc.]

> I'm ending this relationship. It's taken me a long time
> and a lot of courage to be able to say this, but I'm over
> you. You've mistreated me, and I won't tolerate it any
> longer. You've been doing this for years, and you've
> interfered with my growth and well-being. So I'm done.
> I'm walking away, and I won't be coming back. It's not
> me; it's you.

Your letter doesn't need to look like this one. The important thing is that you address it to the part of you that mentally and physically abuses you, that causes you to diet repeatedly or eat compulsively, that causes you to hate your body, which is also part of you, and that has likely been doing this for years, obscuring the real you, and preventing you from being as independent, happy, and fulfilled as you deserve to be.

Then, if you feel up to it, hang this letter on your wall. Store it on your phone. Keep it somewhere on your computer, where you can look at it during the workday. Or send it to me and I will share it, anonymously and with your permission, with other women who need the inspiration to break up with their abusers.

Practice #10: Build an Eat-in-Peace Community
The difficulty with losing the diet, loving your body, and eating in peace is that these are countercultural ideas. Embracing them requires a cultural revolution. Are you willing to revolt?

Good. Now find others to join you. Eating in peace is easier when accomplished in numbers. When we surround ourselves with others who are like-minded, it's easier to stay on track. Conversing about peaceful eating and body love is, essentially, learning a new language, and you'll need peers with whom to practice this tricky, foreign vernacular. Can you seek out friends, family, colleagues, and associates who support your desire to eat in peace and who have made a similar choice for themselves? Just think, your conversations will no longer center around the latest diet or who looks fat and why.

A number of organizations have spearheaded eat-in-peace movements at a national level. For instance, Delta Delta Delta's Fat Talk Free Week is a campaign designed "to draw attention to body image issues and the damaging impact of the 'thin ideal' on women in society."[16] The five-day campaign attempts to illuminate how fat talk negatively impacts our thoughts and feelings about ourselves. Similarly, the Binge Eating Disorder Association sponsors Weight Stigma Awareness Week, to promote education about weight stigma toward the goal of "a world where people are supported in living happy, healthy lives, free of judgment about the size of their bodies."[17]

Beyond these sporadic weeks, can you keep the momentum going, challenging weight discrimination and consciously swimming upstream in a river of constriction, restriction, and self-hate? I encourage you to find a group of women (as large as a national organization or as small as a couple of colleagues or friends) who are willing to take on this task. It's that much easier to experience a shift in thinking and behavior when that shift is normalized among our peers. If you are interested in starting a local Eat-in-Peace discussion group, you can print out various posts from my blog (http://www.everywomanhasaneatingdisorder.blogspot.com) or material from its sister site (http://www.eat-in-peace.com) to kick off your conversations.

Conclusion

Coming to terms with food and your body is a process. It might not be intuitive at this point, given how we're raised, but it's critical to our well-being. You can go through life disliking your body, criticizing it at every glance and degrading it at every opportunity, or accepting it and then moving on to focus on what is ultimately more significant and impactful to you. Switching from the first stance requires practice, effort, and focus (and perhaps near-constant repetition), but it can be done, particularly with community support. Take one step or many. Make the choice to lead a life that nourishes you completely.

℣ Appendix

HERE ARE SOME RESOURCES FOR FURTHER READING.

Size Discrimination

Deb Burgard, Ph.D., "The HAES Files: When Health Speech Is Hate Speech," the Health at Every Size blog, http://healthateverysizeblog .org/2011/09/27/the-haes-files-when-health-speech-is-hate-speech/. In this oft-quoted article, Burgard, writing for the Association for Size Diversity and Health, explains how public health messages targeting fat may actually be size discrimination in disguise.

Abigail Saguy, *What's Wrong with Fat?* (Oxford: Oxford University Press, 2013). Saguy, a sociologist at UCLA, takes a step back from our society's focus on weight and looks at fat through a variety of "frames." Saguy explores, for instance, the relationship between health and weight, weight discrimination, and the fat acceptance movement.

The Well-Rounded Mama, "Terminology," http://wellroundedmama.blogspot .com/p/terminology.html. In this blog entry, the author references the "Health at Every Size" movement and makes a case for using the word "fat" instead of "overweight" and "obese."

Thinness and Anorexia

Marya Hornbacher, *Wasted: A Memoir of Anorexia and Bulimia* (New York: Harper Perennial, 1998). Often, as I note in the book, anorexia is praised and glamorized as a desirable condition. To learn just how dark and painful anorexia can be, read Hornbacher's personal memoir. She rips every little last ounce of glamour from an eating disorder and hangs it out to dry. (Note: Parts of this book may be triggering to those with eating disorders.)

Mara Reinstein, "When 'You're So Skinny!' Is an Insult," *Glamour*, July 1, 2006, http://www.glamour.com/health-fitness/2006/07/skinny-insults. After losing 11 pounds due to enteritis, a gastrointestinal disease, the normally thin Reinstein was surprised by the reactions she received from friends. In this *Glamour* magazine article, she asks, "Why was the outside world so thrilled with my ravaged body?" I'm happy that Reinstein wrote this piece and even happier that she could provide a different (read: healthier) perspective for the fashion industry.

Jennifer J. Thomas and Jenni Schaefer, *Almost Anorexic: Is My (or My Loved One's) Relationship with Food a Problem?* (Center City, MN: Hazelden/Harvard Health Publications, 2013). A collaboration between Thomas, a professor of psychology at Harvard Medical School, and Schaefer, author and speaker and recovery advocate, *Almost Anorexic* elaborates on many of the "every woman" symptoms described in this book. Thomas and Schaefer provide an excellent resource for subthreshold disorders and offer strategies for "kicking ED [overeating disorder] to the curb" and "accepting and loving your body."

Healing Eating

Christopher G. Fairburn, *Overcoming Binge Eating: The Proven Program to Learn Why You Binge and How You Can Stop*, 2nd ed. (New York: Guilford Press, 2013). Fairburn, a professor of psychiatry and director of the Center for Research on Eating Disorders at Oxford University, is an internationally recognized researcher who developed the leading evidenced-based treatment (cognitive-behavioral therapy) for eating disorders. The book is designed for those who struggle with binge eating and can be used as a helpful adjunct to therapy.

Evelyn Tribole and Elyse Resch, *Intuitive Eating: A Revolutionary Program That Works*, 3rd ed. (New York: St. Martin's Griffin, 2012). Tribole and Resch provide the manual for learning how to eat intuitively. The book's ten principles help you to, among other things, "honor your hunger," "respect your fullness," and "reject the diet mentality."

The "Obesity Epidemic" and Health

Glenn Gaesser, *Big Fat Lies: The Truth about Your Weight and Your Health* (Carlsbad, CA: Gurze Books, 2002). While researching his exposé, Gaesser found that obesity is a poor predictor of hypertension (high blood pressure), high cholesterol, hyperlipidemia (high blood fats), and atherosclerosis (clogged arteries). He also found that obese people with type 2 diabetes could improve their health and stop taking medication simply by eating a healthier diet and exercising—no weight loss required. His work also turned up evidence that extra weight might have a positive or preventative effect on common types of cancer, including lung cancer and breast cancer, as well as osteoporosis and certain respiratory diseases.

Gina Kolata, "Diabetes Study Ends Early with a Surprising Result," *New York Times*, October 19, 2012, http://nyti.ms/WMwWKH. In this article, Kolata published the results of an eleven-year study involving more than five thousand participants who were overweight or obese and diagnosed with type 2 diabetes. The study found that participants who were put on a strict diet and exercise schedule did lose weight, but did not have a lower incidence of heart attacks and strokes than those in a control group, indicating that weight loss wasn't related to these health outcomes.

John O'Neil, "Vital Signs: Behavior, the Dangers of Yo-Yo Dieting," the *New York Times*, June 8, 2004, http://www.nytimes.com/2004/06/08/health/vital-signs-behavior-the-dangers-of-yo-yo-dieting.html. Being overweight or obese is not an automatic entry into the disease pool. In fact, where health is concerned, research suggests it may be beneficial to remain at a higher weight, rather than engage in repetitive weight cycling or yo-yo dieting. Disease is more tied to what we eat and how we move than to what we weigh.

For further reading ideas, see the Eat-in-Peace book club, http://www.eat-in-peace.com/book_club, a site I regularly update with new releases that support the Eat-in-Peace message.

Organizations That Can Help

Academy for Eating Disorders (AED), http://aedweb.org/, is a global organization of eating disorder professionals "committed to leadership in eating disorders research, education, treatment, and prevention." The organization disseminates information on eating disorders and promotes best practices across the world. The AED's *International Journal of Eating Disorders* is a widely respected research journal.

Adios Barbie, http://www.adiosbarbie.com/, describes itself as "the body image site for every body" and is focused on "creating a world where everyone is safe and at home with who they are." The site posts articles and resources on body image, eating disorders, and media literacy, all with the intent of saying "adios" to our previous, constricting notions of beauty.

Association for Size Diversity and Health (ASDAH), https://www.sizediversityandhealth.org/Index.asp. ASDAH recognizes that healthy women (and men) come in all shapes and sizes. This organization of professionals works to fight weight and size discrimination by promoting "Health at Every Size" through education, funding science, and sharing findings with the health and fitness industries, as well as policymakers.

Beauty Redefined, http://www.beautyredefined.net/, is an organization that "is dedicated to taking back beauty for females everywhere through teaching people to recognize and reject harmful messages about female bodies in media and cultural discourse." Twin cofounders Lindsay and Lexie write an engaging blog and speak across the country on media and beauty.

Binge Eating Disorder Association (BEDA), http://bedaonline.com/, is a national community formed to help increase awareness about and prevent and treat binge-eating disorder and weight stigma. The organization promotes evidenced-based practices for treating binge eating and is committed to targeting and eliminating size discrimination.

Delta Delta Delta's Body Image 3D, http://bi3d.tridelta.org/, is a "multidimensional approach to body image awareness and education," expanding the definition of a healthy body image to include a healthy mind, body, and spirit. The initiative offers a Body Image Manifesto you can sign and sponsors Fat Talk Free Week and the Reflections: Body Image Program (for college students), among other programming.

Health at Every Size (HAES), http://www.haescommunity.org/, is an online community space founded by nutrition professor and researcher Linda Bacon, PhD, author of *Health at Every Size: The Surprising Truth About Your Weight*, 2nd ed. (Dallas: BenBella Books, 2010). According to the community's website, HAES encourages acceptance of body diversity, intuitive eating, and joyful movement. Practitioners can sign the HAES pledge, and the public can find a provider who practices within the HAES philosophy.

National Eating Disorders Association (NEDA), http://www .nationaleatingdisorders.org/. NEDA is, in the organization's words, "the leading nonprofit organization in the United States advocating on behalf of and supporting individuals and families affected by eating disorders." Its website offers a plethora of information about prevention and treatment. NEDA also sponsors the annual National Eating Disorders Awareness Week (NEDAW), fundraising walks across the country, and offers a toll-free, confidential hotline staffed by trained volunteers at 1-800-931-2237.

Proud2BMe, www.proud2bme.org. Proud2BMe is an online forum created by teens and associated with the National Eating Disorders Association. This website gives teens a place to talk about culture, fashion, entertainment, and news, all while promoting good health and a positive body image. If you're new to the site, I recommend starting with the article, "How Does Social Media Affect Your Body Image?," http://proud2bme.org/node/244.

How to Find a Good Therapist

A number of eating disorder organizations offer lists of providers or online referral finders. Here are a few to start:

Academy for Eating Disorders: http://www.aedweb.org/source /EDProfessional/

Butterfly Foundation: http://thebutterflyfoundation.org.au /%EF%BB%BFneed-help-now/ (for readers in Australia). Also, check out their "Need Help Now" toll-free support line at 1-800-ED-HOPE (1-800-33-4673).

Eating Disorder Hope: http://www.eatingdisorderhope.com/treatment-for -eating-disorders/therapists-specialists

Eating Disorder Referral and Information Center: http://edreferral.com /Referral%20Request.htm

International Association of Eating Disorder Professionals: http://web .memberclicks.com/mc/directory/viewsimplesearch.do?orgId=iaedp

National Eating Disorders Association: http://www.nationaleatingdisorders .org/find-treatment

Once you gather a few names, you may want to call each professional and see how you feel on the phone. It might be useful to speak with several and even to meet more than one for consultation. You'd comparison shop for anything else—don't skimp on your mental health! Above all else, trust your gut. If it doesn't feel right, with time and patience, you'll be able to find someone who does. The "fit," as we say, is key. Here are some questions to ask of a potential therapist:

- Do you specialize in eating disorders? It's important that your therapist know the ins and outs of these disorders. Ask roughly what percentage of her patients have an eating disorder diagnosis—it will give you a sense of how much time each week she spends working with these concerns. Ask if she's received any specific training or education in eating disorders.

- Are you involved in any eating disorder organizations? The answer will help you get a sense of whether the provider is active in the field, up-to-date on research, and interested in the community.

- What is your approach to eating disorder treatment? Ask yourself if you want an active or passive therapist. Do you want to focus on your childhood or what is going on now? You'll want to know if your provider uses approaches that have been shown to work in the research (also known as evidenced-based approaches) like cognitive-behavioral therapy, dialectical-behavioral therapy, or family-based therapy. Other treatment approaches may also be effective, and the quality of the patient-therapist relationship is another factor that may impact treatment success.

- Do you work with a treatment team? Ask what other types of professionals she collaborates with in treating eating disorders. Often, working with eating disorders requires that the patient see a dietician and an internist and that these providers be knowledgeable in eating disorders. Other allied health professionals may join the treatment team, too. Inquire whether she'll be able to provide you with referrals.

- Do you take insurance? You'll want to know if you'll be able to use your mental health benefits to pay for your sessions. Many eating disorder specialists are doing away with managed care due to low reimbursement rates and cumbersome paperwork. If you can afford to pay only a copay, or only have in-network benefits, ask your insurance company to help you find an in-network provider (and go through the above steps to ensure the therapist is adequately resourced to see you). If you're able to pay out of pocket, your therapist can provide you with a billing statement to submit to your insurance company for partial reimbursement. Before you start treatment, however, you may want to call your insurance plan and find out (a) if you have out-of-network benefits, (b) what your deductible is (what you'll have to pay before you start getting reimbursed), (c) if there is a cap on the number of visits your plan will cover, and (d) what percentage of your therapist's services will be reimbursed. (Note: the insurance company may choose to cap reimbursement at a set fee it determines to be customary, which may fall below your therapist's fee; see if you can find out what the customary allowance is.)

 Notes

Preface

1. L. Smolak, *Next Door Neighbors: Eating Disorders Awareness and Prevention Puppet Guide Book* (Seattle: National Eating Disorders Association, 1996).

2. Walter Vandereycken, "Can Eating Disorders Become 'Contagious' in Group Therapy and Specialized Inpatient Care?" *European Eating Disorders Review* 19 (2011): 289–95.

Chapter 1

1. T. D. Wade, A. Keski-Rahkonen, and J. I. Hudson, "Epidemiology of Eating Disorders," in *Textbook of Psychiatric Epidemiology*, 3rd ed., ed. M. T. Tsuang, M. Tohen, and P. B. Jones (New York: Wiley, 2011), 343–60.

2. Anne Bromley, "You Are Not What You Don't Eat: Women's Center's Eating Disorders Program Focuses on Positive and Real Body Images," *UVA Today*, March 4, 2010, http://news.virginia.edu/content/you -are-not-what-you-dont-eat-womens-centers-eating-disorders-program -focuses-positive-%C2%96-and. This statistic has been widely circulated by news outlets and the eating disorders community, but its source is unknown.

3. Minna Rintala and Pertti Mustajoki, "Could Mannequins Menstruate?" *British Medical Journal* 305 (December 19, 1992): 1575–76.

4. Centers for Disease Control and Prevention, "Body Measurements," last updated November 2, 2012, http://www.cdc.gov/nchs/fastats /bodymeas.htm; and J. B. Martin, "The Development of Ideal Body Image Perceptions in the United States," *Nutrition Today* 45, (no. 3) (2010): 98–100.

5. J. I. Hudson, E. Hiripi, H. G. Pope, Jr., and R. C. Kessler, "The Prevalence and Correlates of Eating Disorders in the National Comorbidity Survey Replication," *Biological Psychiatry* 61 (2007): 348–58; R. H. Streigel-Moore and D. L. Franko, "Epidemiology of Binge Eating Disorder," *International Journal of Eating Disorders* 34 Suppl (2003): S19–29; and Wade, et al., "Epidemiology of Eating Disorders." All of these statistics are available online at the National Eating Disorders Association website, http://www.nationaleatingdisorders.org/get-facts-eating-disorders.

6. H. W. Hoek and D. van Hoeken, "Review of the Prevalence and Incidence of Eating Disorders," *International Journal of Eating Disorders* 34, no. 4 (December 2003): 383–96.

7. Sarah Silverman, *Jesus Is Magic*, directed by Liam Lynch (USA: Black Gold Films, 2005).

8. Susie Orbach, *Fat Is a Feminist Issue: The Anti-Diet Guide to Permanent Weight Loss* (New York: Berkeley Books,1978/1979/1990/1994), 70.

9. Nancy Miller, "Meet the New L.A. Ideal," *Los Angeles Magazine*, October 1, 2012, http://www.lamag.com/features-hidden/2012/10/01/meet-the-new-la-ideal1.

10. "The Fitness Body Image Poll," survey conducted by ICR/International Communications Research for *Fitness* magazine, June 2006, http://www.fitnessmagazine.com/health/body-image/stories/the-fitness-body-image-poll/.

11. Ibid.

12. Daniel S. Hamermesh, *Beauty Pays: Why Attractive People Are More Successful* (Princeton, NJ: Princeton University Press, 2011).

13. Abby Ellin, "When the Food Critics Are Deskside," *New York Times*, February 18, 2007, http://www.nytimes.com/2007/02/18/fashion/18Lunch.html?_r=0.

14. Ibid.

15. "Plus Size Bodies, What Is Wrong With Them Anyway?," *Plus Model Magazine & Blog*, January 8, 2012, http://www.plus-model-mag.com/2012/01/plus-size-bodies-what-is-wrong-with-them-anyway/ and "Size 00: Sizes Shrink as Women Get Bigger," Fox News, June 21, 2006, http://www.foxnews.com/story/2006/06/21/size-00-sizes-shrink-as-women-get-bigger/.

16. American Psychiatric Association, "Anorexia Nervosa," in *Diagnostic and Statistical Manual of Mental Disorders*, 5th ed. (*DSM-5*) (Washington, DC: American Psychiatric Association, 2013): 338–39;

American Psychiatric Association, "Bulimia Nervosa," in *DSM-5*, 345–50; and American Psychiatric Association, "OSFED," in *DSM-5*, 353–54. Note: The OSFED classification replaces Eating Disorder Not Otherwise Specified (EDNOS) in the previous version of the manual.

17. Constance Rhodes, *Life Inside the "Thin" Cage: A Personal Look into the Hidden World of the Chronic Dieter* (Colorado Springs, CO: Shaw Books /WaterBrook Press, 2003), 19.

18. Wendy Miller and Edward Ragsdale, "Essential Elements of Change in the Treatment of Eating Disorders: Feminist-Psychoanalytic & Gestalt Theoretical Perspectives," talk presented at the "Addiction Treatment in Metamorphosis: Paragdigm Shift in Theory and Practice" Conference of the Addiction Division of New York State Psychological Association, New York City, April 28, 2006.

Chapter 2

1. David S. Landes, *The Wealth and Poverty of Nations. Why Some Are So Rich and Some Are So Poor* (New York: W. W. Norton & Co., 1999), xix.

2. Jenni Schaefer, *Life Without Ed: How One Woman Declared Independence from Her Eating Disorder and How You Can Too* (New York: McGraw-Hill, 2004), 48.

3. Brenda M. Malinauskas, Thomas D. Raedeke, Victor G. Aeby, Jean L. Smith, and Matthew B. Dallas, "Dieting Practices, Weight Perceptions, and Body Composition: A Comparison of Normal Weight, Overweight, and Obese College Females," *Nutrition Journal* 5, no. 11, (March 31 2006), http://www.nutritionj.com /content/5/1/11 and Christine Hsu, "The Average Woman Spends 17 Years of Her Life on Diets," *Medical Daily*, September 18, 2012, http://www .medicaldaily.com/average-woman-spends-17-years-her-life-diets-242601.

4. Christopher Fairburn, *Overcoming Binge Eating* (New York: The Guilford Press, 1995), 44–45.

5. Heidi Michels Blanck, Laura Kettel Khan, and Mary K. Serdula, "Use of Nonprescription Weight Loss Products—Results from a Multistate Survey," *Journal of the American Medical Association* 286, no. 8, (2001): 930–35.

6. H. M. Connolly, J. L. Crary, M. D. McGoon, D. D. Hensrud, B. S. Edwards, W. D. Edwards, and H. V. Schaff, "Valvular Heart Disease Associated with Fenfluramine—Phentermine," *New England Journal of Medicine* 337 (9) (1997): 581–88; Lawrence Bachorik, "FDA Announces Withdrawal Fenfluramine and Dexfenfluramine (Fen-Phen),"

press release, U.S. Food and Drug Administration, September 15, 1997 http://www.fda.gov/Drugs/DrugSafety/PostmarketDrugSafetyInformationforPatientsandProviders/ucm179871.htm.

7. D. Samenuk, M. S. Link, M. K. Homoud, R. Contreras, T. C. Theoharides, P. J. Wang, and N. A. Estes III, "Adverse Cardiovascular Events Temporally Associated with Ma Huang, an Herbal Source of Ephedrine," *Mayo Clinic Proceedings* 77, no. 1, (2002): 12–16; "FDA Acts to Remove Ephedra-Containing Dietary Supplements from Market," press release, U.S. Food and Drug Administration, November 23, 2004, http://www.fda.gov/NewsEvents/Newsroom/PressAnnouncements/2004/ucm108379.htm.

8. Carla Hall, "New Diet Drug Touches Off a Feeding Frenzy," *Los Angeles Times*, June 15, 2007, http://www.latimes.com/news/obituaries/la-me-dietdrug15jun15,0,5820307.story.

9. "FAQs," Alli website, http://www.myalli.com/FAQs/treatment-effects/.

10. "HCG Diet Products Are Illegal" consumer update, U.S. Food and Drug Administration December 26, 2011, http://www.fda.gov/forconsumers/consumerupdates/ucm281333.htm.

11. "Rare and Severe Liposuction Complications," http://www.liposuction.com/rare-complications.html.

12. Todd Tucker, *The Great Starvation Experiment: Ancel Keys and the Men Who Starved for Science* (Minneapolis: First University of Minnesota Press, 2006).

13. With regard to the current discussion, I am not referring to those compulsive exercisers who participate with rigidity in order to manage mood states, such as anxiety or depression, but rather those who are unable to miss a workout due to ideas about weight and shape.

14. Caroline Knapp, *Drinking: A Love Story* (New York: Bantam Dell, 1996), 56-57.

15. *Will & Grace*, "A Gay/December Romance," episode 612, January 2, 2004, directed by James Barrows.

16. Elyse Resch, "Member Viewpoint: The Sadness of Saying 'Enough,'" *The Academy for Eating Disorders Newsletter* 17 (3), http://www.aedweb.org/source/newsletter/index.cfm?fuseaction=Newsletter.showThisIssue&Issue_ID=12&Article_ID=239.

17. Geneen Roth, "The Toss-Your-Scale Diet Plan," *Good Housekeeping*, June 1, 2007, http://www.goodhousekeeping.com/health/diet-plans/toss-scale-diet-jun07.

18. Shaun Dreisbach, "Shocking Body-Image News: 97% of Women Will Be Cruel to Their Bodies Today," *Glamour* magazine, February 2011, http://www.glamour.com/health-fitness/2011/02/shocking-body-image-news-97-percent-of-women-will-be-cruel-to-their-bodies-today.

19. Leslie Goldman, personal communication (interview), September 14, 2007.

20. Golda Poretsky, "Why It's Okay to Be Fat: A Story of Self-Acceptance," TEDxMillRiver talk, 2012, http://proud2bme.org/content/video-why-its-okay-be-fat-story-self-acceptance.

21. Roth, 2007.

22. Vivian Diller, "The Challenges of Aging in Today's Culture," *Psychology Today*, September 11, 2012, http://www.psychologytoday.com/blog/face-it/201209/some-women-try-mirror-fasting.

Chapter 3

1. Basic Research ad.

2. Jean Kilbourne, *Killing Us Softly 3: Advertising's Images of Women*, produced by Sut Jhally, Media Education Foundation, 1999.

3. "The Fabric of Our Lives" campaign, Cotton, Incorporated (1989).

4. "Weightless: A Short Story," Special K campaign, General Mills, 2006.

5. Yoplait Light campaign, Yoplait USA, Inc., 2006, http://www.splendad.com/ads/show/936-Yoplait-Light-Raft-Yellow-Polka-Dot-Bikini.

6. fatgirlslim campaign, Bliss brand, carried by Sephora, Inc.

7. Slim-Fast Optima Shakes campaign, Unilever, 2007.

8. "New Beauty Study Reveals Days, Times and Occasions When U.S. Women Feel Least Attractive," PHD Media, news release, October 2, 2013, http://www.prnewswire.com/news-releases/new-beauty-study-reveals-days-times-and-occasions-when-us-women-feel-least-attractive-226131921.html.

9. Chana Ya'ar, "Knesset Passes New Anorexia Law," Israel National News, March 20, 2012, http://www.israelnationalnews.com/News/News.aspx/153937#.UksEOmiYaRh.

10. "Respect Yourself in the Morning," Nutri-Grain advertisement, The Kellogg Company, Inc., 2002.

11. PR Newswire, "Green Giant Announces 'Giant Difference Campaign' Aimed at Diet Cheaters," September 29, 2013, http://www .marketwatch.com/story/green-giant-announces-giant-difference -campaign-aimed-at-diet-cheaters-2013-09-19-15183270. Jean Kilbourne discusses the advertising industry's portrayal of food as a moral/sexual issue in her film *Slim Hopes: Advertising & the Obsession with Thinness*, 1995, produced and directed by Sut Jhally, and in her book *Can't Buy My Love: How Advertising Changes the Way We Think and Feel* (New York: Touchstone, 1999), 113–116.

12. Paul Campos, *The Diet Myth: Why America's Obsession with Weight Is Hazardous to Your Health* (New York: Gotham Books, 2004), 97.

13. Dairy Queen, A.M.D.Q. Corporation.

14. Harriet Hall, "Akavar 20/50 and Truth in Advertising," *Science Based Medicine*, January 22, 2008, http://www.sciencebasedmedicine.org /akavar-2050-and-truth-in-advertising/.

15. *Family Guy*, "Chitty Chitty Death Bang," episode 103, April 20, 1998, executive produced by Seth MacFarlane and David Zuckerman.

16. Whitney Cummings, "101 Incredible Celebrity Slimdowns," March 13, 2006, produced by Matt Holthaus of E!

17. "Blondorexia," *Urban Dictionary*, http://www.urbandictionary.com /define.php?term=Blondorexia.

18. "50 Most Shocking Celebrity Confessions," June 3, 2010, produced by E! Transcript available online at http://livedash.ark.com/transcript /50_most_shocking_celebrity_confessions/6834/EP/Thursday_June _03_2010/320300/.

19. "Statistics: How Many People Have Eating Disorders?," Anorexia Nervosa and Related Eating Disorders (ANRED) website, accessed http://www.anred.com/stats.html.

20. Todd Peterson, "Dennis Quaid: I Battled Anorexia," *People*, March 10, 2006, http://www.people.com/people/article/0,,1172023,00.html.

21. Debra Anscombe Wood, RN, "'Anorexia as Lifestyle' Gains Momentum," July 31, 2006, http://news.nurse.com/apps/pbcs.dll /article?AID=2006607310340#.UlA2vMY709Y. The original pro-ana website in question is no longer active.

22. "Craving Thin," http://cravingthin.weebly.com/food.html.

23. Charlotte Andersen, "Is 'Fitspiration' Really Any Better Than 'Thinspiration'?" *The Great Fitness Experiment*, February 26, 2012, http://www.thegreatfitnessexperiment.com/2012/02/is-fitspiration-really -any-better-than-thinspiration.html.

24. "Skinny S.O.S.! Stars' Scary New Affliction—Foodophobia and It's Contagious!" *Star Magazine*, July 10, 2006.

25. Doris Smeltzer with Andrea Lynn Smeltzer, *Andrea's Voice: Silenced by Bulimia: Her Story and Her Mother's Journey through Grief and Understanding* (Carlsbad, CA: Gurze, 2006), 34.

26. *Zagat Guide*, 2006.

27. Jessica Weiner, *Do I Look Fat in This? Life Doesn't Begin Five Pounds from Now* (New York: Simon Spotlight Entertainment/Simon & Schuster, 2006), 3.

28. Ibid., 46.

29. Ibid., 189.

Chapter 4

1. Lynn Hirschberg, "A Film of One's Own," *New York Times*, September 2, 2006, http://www.nytimes.com/2006/09/03/magazine /03actesses.html?_r=2&pagewanted=all.

2. Lynda G. Boothroyd, Martin J. Tovée, and Thomas V. Pollet, "Visual Diet versus Associative Learning as Mechanisms of Change in Body Size Preferences," *PLoS ONE* 7, no. 11 (2012): e48691.

3. "Mariah on Morsel Diet," Mariah Carey Archives, http://www .mcarchives.com/index.asp?id=5721.

4. Melissa Whitworth, "Victoria's Secret Show: What Does It Take to Be a Victoria's Secret Angel?" *Telegraph*, last modified November 7, 2011, http://fashion.telegraph.co.uk/news-features/TMG8872623/Victorias -Secret-show-What-does-it-take-to-be-a-Victorias-Secret-Angel.html.

5. Rob Medich, "Does American Idol Have a Body Bias?" *Idol News*, last modified March 30, 2006, http://z12.invisionfree.com/Your _American_Idol/ar/t38.htm.

6. "Nicole Richie: The Ultimate Transformation," YouTube video, uploaded July 5, 2008, http://www.youtube.com/watch?v =9mG5E6HWd44.

7. "Which Emaciated Star Will Disappear First?" reader poll, *The Hollywood Gossip*, created August 18, 2006, http://www .thehollywoodgossip.com/polls/which-emaciated-star-will-disappear-first .html.

8. "Kelly Clarkson Was Bulimic," The Superficial, last modified June 21, 2007, http://www.thesuperficial.com/kelly_clarkson_was _bulimic-06-2007.

9. Holly Millea, "Why Fat Is Back in Hollywood," *Details*, last modified July 2006, http://www.details.com/culture-trends/critical -eye/200607/why-women-with-some-meat-on-their-bones-are-rising-to -the-top.

10. Ibid.

11. Jennifer Aniston, BrainyQuote.com, http://www.brainyquote .com/quotes/quotes/j/jenniferan401659.html#KGJX5bXyJ6AQhz7j.99; Karen Borsari and Margaret Hartmann, "Rosario Dawson: Body Pressure on Women Is 'A Form of Violence,'" *Jezebel*, July 28, 2011, http://jezebel .com/5825516/rosario-dawson—body-pressure-on-women-is-a-form-of -violence; Amy Larocca, "Woman of the Hourglass," *New York*, February 14, 2010, http://nymag.com/fashion/10/spring/63808/.

12. Jay Allen, "Sandra Bullock: I'm Not Pregnant! So Stop Asking!" *Parent Dish*, last modified October 27, 2005, http://www.parentdish .com/2005/10/27/sandra-bullock-im-not-pregnant-so-stop-asking/.

13. "Study Finds Young Women's Satisfaction with Own Body Image Suffers after Viewing Ultra-thin TV Characters," Ryerson University, last modified August 14, 2009, http://www.ryerson.ca/news/news/Research _News/20090814_Want.html.

14. "Attack of the Five Foot Ten Woman," *Sex and the City*, June 18, 2000, directed by Pam Thomas.

15. John Millar, "TV Bosses Said I Was Too Fat...So I Bought a Bag of Cookies; How Weight Jibes Drove Sex and the City's Kristin Davis to Binge on Snacks," *Scottish Daily & Sunday Mail* (Glasgow, Scotland), March 19, 2006.

16. Jeannette Walls, "Scientology Foes Blast Cruise in Ad—Plus: Kristin Davis Weighs in on Pressure to Be Thin in TV," *Today*, last modified March 29, 2006, http://www.today.com/id/11878503#.UtXHp55dV8G.

17. *Life & Style Magazine*, March 26, 2012, 47.

Chapter 5

1. Marketdata Enterprises: "Weight Loss Market in U.S. Up 1.7% to $61 Billion," PR Web, April 16, 2013, http://www.prweb.com /releases/2013/4/prweb10629316.htm.

2. Dianne Neumark-Sztainer, Melanie Wall, Mary Story, and Amber R. Standish, "Dieting and Unhealthy Weight Control Behaviors During Adolescence: Associations with 10-Year Changes in Body Mass Index," *Journal of Adolescent Health* 50, no. 1 (January 2012): 80–86.

3. Traci Mann, A. Janet Tomiyama, Erika Westling, Ann-Marie Lew, Barbra Samuels, and Jason Chatman, "Medicare's Search for Effective Obesity Treatments: Diets Are Not the Answer," *American Psychologist* 62, no. 3 (April, 2007): 220–33.

4. "Why Your Brain Doesn't Want You to Lose Weight: Sandra Aamodt at TEDGlobal 2013," last modified June 11, 2013, http://blog.ted .com/2013/06/11/why-your-brain-doesnt-want-you-to-lose-weight-sandra -aamodt-at-tedglobal-2013/.

5. Gary D. Foster, Holly R. Wyatt, James O. Hill, Brian G. McGuckin, Carrie Brill, Selma Mohammed, Philippe O. Szapary, Daniel J. Rader, Joel S. Edman, and Samuel Klein, "A Randomized Trial of a Low-Carbohydrate Diet for Obesity," *New England Journal of Medicine* 348 (May 22, 2003): 2082–90.

6. Gina Kolata, *Rethinking Thin: The New Science of Weight Loss—and the Myths and Realities of Dieting* (New York: Farrar, Straus and Giroux, 2007) 217.

7. Linda Bacon, Judith S. Stern, Marta D. Van Loan, and Nancy L. Keim, "Size Acceptance and Intuitive Eating Improve Health for Obese, Female Chronic Dieters," *Journal of the American Dietetic Association* 105, no. 6 (June 2005): 929–36.

8. Kolata, *Rethinking Thin*, 219.

9. Ibid., 221.

10. Atkins Diet financials, 2008, www.galegroup.com/essentials /company/1289361?u=down546633 (available through library subscription service only); The South Beach Diet financials, undated, http://www.manta.com/c/mtr3823/south-beach-diet; The Zone Diet financials, undated, http://www.manta.com/c/mmyjzcy/zone-labs-inc; Jenny Craig financials (subsidiary of Nestle), Nutrisystem Inc. 2012 financials, *Bloomberg Businessweek*, http://investing.businessweek.com /research/stocks/earnings/earnings.asp?ticker=NTRI.

11. "Weight Watchers Monthly Pass," Weight Watchers, http://www .weightwatchers.com/monthlypass/.

12. Weight Watchers International, Inc. 2012 financials, *Bloomberg Businesweek*, http://investing.businessweek.com/research/stocks/earnings /earnings.asp?ticker=WTW.

13. Campos, *The Diet Myth*, xxv.

14. A. Romero-Corral, V. M. Montori, V. K. Somers, J. Korinek, R. J. Thomas, T. G. Allison, F. Mookadam, and F. Lopez-Jimenez, "Association of Bodyweight with Total Mortality and with Cardiovascular Events in

Coronary Artery Disease: A Systematic Review of Cohort Studies," *Lancet* 368 (August 19, 2006): 666–78.

15. "Metabolic Syndrome," Mayo Clinic website, last modified April 2013, http://www.mayoclinic.com/health/metabolic%20syndrome /DS00522.

16. Rachel P. Wildman, Paul Muntner, Kristi Reynolds, Aileen P. McGinn, Swapnil Rajpathak, Judith Wylie-Rosett, and MaryFran R. Sowers, "The Obese without Cardiometabolic Risk Factor Clustering and the Normal Weight with Cardiometabolic Risk Factor Clustering Prevalence and Correlates of 2 Phenotypes among the US Population (NHANES 1999-2004)," *The Archives of Internal Medicine* 168, no. 15 (2008): 1617–24.

17. Harriet Brown, "In 'Obesity Paradox,' Thinner May Mean Sicker," *New York Times*, September 17, 2012, http://www.nytimes .com/2012/09/18/health/research/more-data-suggests-fitness-matters -more-than-weight.html?ref=science.

18. Katherine M. Flegal, "Excess Deaths Associated with Underweight, Overweight, and Obesity," *Journal of the American Medical Association* 293, no. 15 (April 20, 2005): 1861–67.

19. Katherine M. Flegal, Brian K. Kit, Heather Orpana, and Barry I. Graubard, "Association of All-Cause Mortality with Overweight and Obesity Using Standard Body Mass Index Categories: A Systematic Review and Meta-analysis," *Journal of the American Medical Association* 309, no. 1 (January 2, 2013): 71–82.

20. Glenn Gaesser, *Big Fat Lies: The Truth About Your Weight and Your Health* (Carlsbad, CA: Gurze Books, 2002).

21. Abigail Saguy, *What's Wrong with Fat?* (Oxford: Oxford University Press, 2013), 140.

22. "Obesity and Overweight Data," Centers for Disease Control and Prevention, last updated May 30, 2013, http://www.cdc.gov/nchs/fastats /overwt.htm; "Obesity and Overweight Fact Sheet," World Health Organization, last updated March 2013, http://www.who.int/mediacentre /factsheets/fs311/en/.

23. Campos, *The Diet Myth*, xxiv.

24. Marya Hornbacher, *Wasted: A Memoir of Anorexia and Bulimia* (New York: Harper Perennial, 1998), 149 (footnote on page).

25. Campos, *The Diet Myth*, xxi.

26. S. Yusuf, S. Hawken, S. Ounpuu, L. Bautista, M. G. Franzosi, P. Commerford, C. C. C. Lang, Z. Rumboldt, C. L. Onen, L. Lisheng,

S. Tanomsup, P. Wangai Jr., F. Razak, A. M. Sharma, and S. S. Anand, "Obesity and the Risk of Myocardial Infarction in 27,000 Participants from 52 Countries: A Case-Control Study," *Lancet* 366, no. 9497 (November 5, 2005): 1640–49.

27. Kolata, *Rethinking Thin*.

28. Ibid., 223.

29. "Weight Bias at Home and School," video, Yale Rudd Center for Food Policy & Obesity, http://www.yaleruddcenter.org/what_we _do.aspx?id=254.

30. R. M. Puhl, T. Andreyeva, and K. D. Brownell, "Perceptions of Weight Discrimination: Prevalence and Comparison to Race and Gender Discrimination in America," *International Journal of Obesity* 32, no. 6 (June 2008): 1–9.

31. J. D. Latner, D. S. Ebneter, and K. S. O'Brien, "Residual Obesity Stigma: an Experimental Investigation of Bias against Obese and Lean Targets Differing in Weight-Loss History," *Obesity* 20, no. 10 (October, 2012): 2035–38.

32. Judith Moore, *Fat Girl: A True Story* (New York: Plume, 2005), 1–2.

33. Ibid., 7.

34. Georgia's Strong4Life Campaign Relies Heavily on Fat-Shaming," February 7, 2012, http://www.about-face.org/georgias-strong4life -campaign-relies-heavily-on-fat-shaming/. You can see the current Strong4Life campaign online at their website, http://strong4life.com/.

35. Gina Kolata, "For a World of Woes, We Blame Cookie Monsters," *New York Times*, October 29, 2006, http://www.nytimes.com/2006/10/29 /weekinreview/29kolata.html.

36. Ross A. Hammond and Ruth Levine, "The Economic Impact of Obesity in the United States," *Diabetes and Metabolic Syndrome and Obesity: Targets and Therapy* 3 (2010): 285–95.

37. Kolata, "We Blame Cookie Monsters."

38. "Health at Every Size Fact Sheet," Association for Size Diversity and Health, updated October 20, 2011, https://wwwsizediversityandhealth .org/content.asp?id=161.

39. Kolata, "We Blame Cookie Monsters."

Chapter 6

1. Schaefer, *Life Without Ed*, 76.

2. *Little Miss Sunshine,* directed by Jonathan Dayton and Valerie Faris (USA: Fox Searchlight Pictures, 2006).

3. Pam Houston, *A Little More About Me* (New York: Washington Square Press, 1999), 160.

4. "Good Shit Lollipop," *Weeds*, Season 1, Episode 3 (USA: Lions Gate Television, August 22, 2005).

5. Kyung E. Rhee, Julie C. Lumeng, Danielle P. Appugliese, Niko Kaciroti, and Robert H. Bradley, "Parenting Styles and Overweight Status in First Grade," *Pediatrics* 117, no. 6 (2006): 2047–54.

6. Jennifer A. Harriger, Rachel M. Calogero, David. C. Witherington, and Jane Ellen Smith, "Body Size Stereotyping and Internalization of the Thin Ideal in Preschool Girls," *Sex Roles* 63 (2010): 609–20.

7. Liz Vaccariello, "The Biggest Loser: A Mother/Daughter Affair?" *Prevention*, last updated March 28, 2008, http://shine.yahoo.com/healthy-living/the-biggest-loser-a-mother-daughter-affair-153160.html.

8. Leslie Goldman, personal communication, September 14, 2007.

9. Liz Funk, *Supergirls Speak Out: Inside the Secret Crisis of Overachieving Girls* (New York: Touchstone/A Division of Simon & Schuster, 2009), 9.

10. Ibid., 15.

11. Marla E. Eisenberg and Dianne Neumark-Sztainer, "Friends' Dieting and Disordered Eating Behaviors Among Adolescents Five Years Later: Findings from Project EAT," *Journal of Adolescent Health* 47, no. 1 (July 2010): 67–73.

12. "Freshman 15," Cornell University Gannett Health Services, accessed September 23, 2013, http://www.gannett.cornell.edu/topics/nutrition/info/freshman15.cfm.

13. Ibid.

14. James I. Hudson, Eva Hiripi, Harrison G. Pope, Jr., and Ronald C. Kessler, "The Prevalence and Correlates of Eating Disorders in the National Comorbidity Survey Replication," *Biological Psychiatry* 61, no. 3 (February 1, 2007): 348–58.

15. Kendra Lee, "Op/Ed: Mind What You're Wearing, Not What They're Eating," *Eagle*, modified February 5, 2013, http://www.theeagleonline.com/opinion/story/mind-what-youre-wearing-not-what-theyre-eating2/.

16. Alexandra Robbins, *Pledged: The Secret Life of Sororities* (New York: Hyperion, 2004), 33.

17. Ibid., 153.

18. Margaret Anne Rose, *Rush: A Girl's Guide to Sorority Success* (New York: Villard Books, 1985). The quote in question appears on page 224 in the Robbins book, *Pledged: The Secret Life of Sororities*.

19. Robbins, *Pledged*, 259.

20. S. M. Platek and D. Singh, "Optimal Waist-to-Hip Ratios in Women Activate Neural Reward Centers in Men," *PLoS ONE* 5 (2) (2010): e9042, http://www.plosone.org/article/info:doi/10.1371/journal.pone.0009042.

21. Johan C. Karremans, Willem E. Frankenhuis, and Sander Arons, "Blind Men Prefer a Low Waist-to-Hip Ratio," *Evolution and Human Behavior* 31 (2010): 182–86.

22. B. M. Zaadstra, J. C. Seidell, P. A. Van Noord, E. R. te Velde, J. D. Habbema, B. Vrieswijk, and J. Karbaat, "Fat and Female Fecundity: Prospective Study of Effect of Body Fat Distribution on Conception Rates," *British Medical Journal* 306 (February 20, 1993): 484–87.

23. Liz Funk, "Sex & the Curvy Girl," YourTango.com, http://www.yourtango.com/20085282/sex-the-curvy-girl?alt=3.

24. Carol L. Glasser, Belinda Robnett, and Cynthia Feliciano, "Internet Daters' Body Type Preferences: Race-Ethnic and Gender Differences," *Sex Roles* 61, no. 1–2 (July 2009): 14–33.

25. Abby Ellin, "Wedding Weight-Loss Madness," *Modern Bride* (Feb/March 2009): 450–53.

26. Ibid., 451.

27. Susan S. Lang, "The Bride Wore White, and, Maybe, Less Weight—But Study Shows She May Have Gone to Extremes for That Svelte Look," *Cornell Chronicle*, January 23, 2008, http://www.news.cornell.edu/stories/2008/01/wedding-day-weight-wishes-lose-more-20-pounds.

28. Ellin, "Wedding Weight-Loss Madness," 450–53.

29. Dodai Stewart, "Just Shut the Fuck Up About Kim Kardashian's Weight," Jezebel.com, last updated March 22, 2013, http://jezebel.com/5991890/just-shut-the-fuck-up-about-kim-kardashians-weight.

30. Annie Murphy Paul, "Too Fat and Pregnant," *New York Times*, last modified July 13, 2008, http://www.nytimes.com/2008/07/13/magazine/13wwln-essay-t.html?_r=0.

31. Tracy Moore, "Do I Look Like a Mom? No Really, You Can Tell Me," Jezebel.com, http://jezebel.com/5946715/do-i-look-like-a-mom-no-really-you-can-tell-me.

32. Danielle A. Gagne, Ann Von Holle, Kimberly A. Brownley, Cristin D. Runfola, Sara Hofmeier, Kateland E. Branch, and Cynthia M. Bulik, "Eating Disorder Symptoms and Weight and Shape Concerns in a Large Web-based Convenience Sample of Women Ages 50 and Above: Results of

the Gender and Body Image (GABI) Study," *International Journal of Eating Disorders* 45 (2012): 832–44.

33. Joan Chrisler, "Body Image Issues of Women Over 50," in *Women Over 50: Psychological Perspectives*, ed. Varda Muhlbauer and Joan C. Chrisler (Springer, 2007), 6.

34. Claire Mysko and Magali Amadei, *Does This Pregnancy Make Me Look Fat? The Essential Guide to Loving Your Body Before and After Baby* (Deerfield Beach: Health Communications, Inc., 2009).

Chapter 7

1. American Psychiatric Association, "Anorexia Nervosa," in *DSM-5*, 341; American Psychiatric Association, "Bulimia Nervosa," in *DSM-5*, 347; and American Psychiatric Association, "Binge-Eating Disorder," in *DSM-5*, 351.

2. Susan Brownmiller, *Femininity* (New York: Ballantine Books, 1985), 25.

3. Kilbourne, *Killing Us Softly 3*.

4. Lindsey Hall and Leigh Cohn, *Bulimia: A Guide to Recovery* (Carlsbad, CA: Gurze Books, 2011), 38–41.

5. Larry Rohter, "In the Land of Bold Beauty, a Trusted Mirror Cracks," *New York Times*, January 14, 2007, http://www.nytimes.com/2007/01/14 /weekinreview/14roht.html?pagewanted=all&_r=0.

6. John Percy, "London 2012 Olympics: Brazil's Women Footballers Labelled Too Fat to Win Gold at Games by Defeated Coach," *Telegraph*, July 26, 2012, http://www.telegraph.co.uk/sport/olympics/football /9430979/London-2012-Olympics-Brazils-women-footballers -labelled-too-fat-to-win-gold-at-Games-by-defeated-coach.html.

7. Carol Tavris, *The Mismeasure of Woman: Why Women Are Not the Better Sex, the Inferior Sex, or the Opposite Sex* (New York: Simon & Schuster, 1992), 17.

8. American Psychiatric Association, "Conversion Disorder (Functional Neurological Symptom Disorder)," 320.

9. Ibid., 16.

10. Naomi Wolf, *The Beauty Myth: How Images of Beauty Are Used Against Women* (New York: Harper Perennial, 2002, 1991), 232.

11. Kjerstin Gruys, *Mirror, Mirror Off the Wall: How I Learned to Love My Body by Not Looking at It for a Year* (New York: Penguin, 2013), 130.

12. Wolf, *The Beauty Myth*, 10.

13. Hall and Cohn, *Bulimia*, 38–41.

14. Julie Zeilinger, "Why Millennial Women Do Not Want to Lead," Forbes.com, last modified July 26, 2012, http://www.forbes.com/sites/deniserestauri/2012/07/16/why-millennial-women-do-not-want-to-lead/.

15. Top Dietitians of the American Diabetic Association, "100 Smartest Diet Tips Ever," Prevention.com, November 2011, http://www.prevention.com/weight-loss/weight-loss-tips/diet-and-healthy-weight-loss-advice?page=3.

16. Pam Houston, *A Little More About Me* (New York: Washington Square Press, 1999), 157.

17. Leslie Goldman, personal communication, September 14, 2007.

Chapter 8

1. J. O. Prochaska, J. C. Norcross, and C. C. DiClemente. *Changing for Good: The Revolutionary Program That Explains the Six Stages of Change and Teaches You How to Free Yourself from Bad Habits* (New York: William Morrow, 1994), 38–46.

2. David Keeps, "Get a Peek Inside Cindy Crawford's Home," *Redbook*, http://www.redbookmag.com/fun-contests/celebrity/cindy-crawford-interview-3.

3. Campos, *The Diet Myth*.

4. Louise Story, "Anywhere the Eye Can See, It's Likely to See an Ad," *New York Times*, January 15, 2007, http://www.nytimes.com/2007/01/15/business/media/15everywhere.html?pagewanted=all&_r=0.

5. Evelyn Tribole & Elyse Resch, *Intuitive Eating: A Revolutionary Program That Works*, 3rd ed. (New York: St. Martin's Griffin, 2012).

6. Jane Hirschmann and Carol Munter, *Overcoming Overeating: How to Break the Diet/Binge Cycle and Live a Healthier, More Satisfying Life* (Philadelphia: Da Capo Press/Perseus Books Group, 2008).

7. Karen Horney, *Neurosis and Human Growth: The Struggle Toward Self-Realization* (New York: W. W. Norton & Co., 1950).

8. "Ralph Waldo Emerson Biography," IMDb, http://www.imdb.com/name/nm0256248/bio.

9. Jason Luoma, Steven Hayes, and Robyn Walser, *Learning ACT: An Acceptance and Commitment Therapy Skills Training Manual for Therapists* (Oakland, CA: New Harbinger Publications, 2007), 135.

10. Janet Buckworth & Rodney Dishman, "Exercise Adherence" in *Handbook of Sport Psychology*, 3rd ed. Gershon Tenenbaum & Robert C. Ecklund, eds. (Hoboken, NJ: John Wiley & Sons, 2007): 509–36.

11. Jon Kabat-Zinn, *Full Catastrophe Living: Using the Wisdom of Your Body and Mind to Face Stress, Pain, and Illness* (New York: Delta Trade Paperbacks, Division of Random House, 1990).

12. Brian Wansink and Koert van Ittersum, "Fast Food Restaurant Lighting and Music Can Reduce Calorie Intake and Increase Satisfaction," *Psychological Reports* 111, no. 1 (2012): 228–32.

13. Rachael Rettner, "Wild Stock Market Could Make You Eat More," NBC News, updated August 23, 2011, http://www.nbcnews.com /id/44248185/ns/health-diet_and_nutrition/t/wild-stock-market-could -make-you-eat-more/#.Ukc8gMY709Z.

14. "Fat Talk Free Week," BodyImage3D website, http://bi3d.tridelta .org/ourinitiatives/fattalkfreeweek.

15. "Weight Stigma Awareness Week—About," Binge Eating Disorder Association (BEDA), http://bedaonline.com/weight-stigma-awareness -week-about/#.Ukc-ecY709Y.

16. Thomas Cash, *The Body Image Workbook: An 8-step Program for Learning to Like Your Looks* (Oakland, CA: New Harbinger, 1997).

17. Schaefer, *Life Without Ed*, 5–6.

Index

M

marketing practices, 39

market research, 138

marriage, 110–111

Mayo Clinic, 81

meaning, finding, 151

media. *See also* advertising; celebrity worship; models

becoming an intelligent consumer, 136–138

celebrity body gossip in, 55–56

comments and jokes in entertainment about size and shape, 42–44

controlling consumption of celebrity, 66

themes of celebrity weeklies, 55

too-fat/too-thin celebrities, 58–59

men's issues, 106, 108–109, 110, 117–118, 124–125, 130

mental energy, redirecting, 11

metabolic syndrome, 81

Millea, Holly, 61–62

Miller, Wendy, 11

mindfulness, 152–153

Minnesota starvation study, 23, 24

Mirror, Mirror, Off the Wall: How I Learned to Love My Body by Not Looking at It for a Year (Gruys), 126

mirror checking, compulsive, 32–34

mirror desensitization, 156

The Mismeasure of Woman: Why Women Are Not the Better Sex, the Inferior Sex, or the Opposite Sex (Tavris), 122

modeling self-critical behaviors, 96

models. *See also* celebrity worship; media

Israel's law on advertising with, 40

measures taken for thinness by, 66

plus-size, 66

selling thinness by, 56

size of, 8–9

supermodels, 57

truth about appearances, 136

Moore, Judith, 86, 87–88

Moore, Tracy, 114

mortality rates, obesity and, 82, 84

motivation, for exercise, 26

Munter, Carol, 143

music industry, thin bias of, 59

N

National Eating Disorders Association (NEDA), 39–40

ambassadors to, 65

negativity

brainwashing, 125

counteracting, 99

outside the home, 101–102

New York Times, 81–82, 87, 119

"When the Food Critics Are Deskside," 8

New York Times Magazine, 55–56

nonjudgmental acceptance, 153–154

normal-weight adults, 81

normal women, perceptions of, 122–125

norms, male and female body, 124

nourishing your life, 143–144

nurturing yourself, 143–144

Nutrition Journal, 15

/// Acknowledgments

I'M GRATEFUL TO A LARGE CIRCLE OF WOMEN who helped me bring this book to print. To my blogging audience, commenters, and friends, I never would have had the incentive to write or material to proceed with the book if not for the online community I joined and the following I developed. Thank you to each and every person who read my blog, commented on it, e-mailed me privately, met me in person, shared her story, and, as a whole, encouraged my writing and my blog. Special thanks to the women who gave me permission to print their stories here.

To the folks over at Healthline and Eating Disorder Hope who awarded my blog top eating disorder honors (naming it one of the Best Eating Disorder Blogs and the Top 25 Eating Disorder Blogs, respectively) and those at Wellsphere, who early in my blogging days named me a Top Health Blogger.

To Sharon Goldinger, Kristen Havens, and Rodi Rosensweig, all bright and talented women whose varying skill sets helped bring this project to fruition.

To my grandmother, Elaine Fischer, a sharp, passionate woman who was always in my corner, who inspired my early love for words, giving me spelling challenges long after others tired out, and whose legacy lives on in part in my love for all things verbal. I have a feeling she'd be selling my book door-to-door if she were here.

To my mother, Cathy Fischer Rosenfeld, who gave me writing assignments on rainy days when I was young, who shares my commitment to the turn of a perfect phrase, and who always told me I should do something with my writing. I love you beyond words.

To Callie, my canine love, who yet again waited patiently by my feet as I churned out another project. She eats with gusto and is blissfully unaware of her physique, a model for us all.

To my writing teachers, my eating disorder and general therapy mentors, my colleagues and patients, family and friends, you each did your part in shaping the way I eat, think, write, and practice therapy. I'm thrilled to see my first book in print.

⁂ About the Author

DR. STACEY ROSENFELD is a clinical psychologist who is committed to helping people develop healthier relationships with food and their bodies. She began writing her *Does Every Woman Have an Eating Disorder?* blog in 2006 to share her ideas and open up a conversation with women about their fixation on their weight, shape, or eating, and the site quickly developed a large following. It has won multiple awards and is included in Healthline's list of the Best Eating Disorder Blogs and Eating Disorder Hope's list of the Top 25 Eating Disorder Blogs.

Dr. Rosenfeld lectures around the country on her "Lose the Diet. Love Your Body. Eat in Peace." philosophy and has appeared on television shows such as *Today*, *ABC News*, and the *Dr. Oz Show*. In addition to her work with eating disorders and body image, she works with patients who have substance abuse problems, anxiety and mood disorders, and relationship difficulties. A certified group psychotherapist, she has worked at treatment centers and universities as well as in private practice.

She is also certified as a personal trainer and indoor cycling instructor and previously served as the chief psychologist of the New York City Triathlon. She encourages people to re-create the role that physical activity had in their lives as children, returning to movement for fun and to help them improve their physical and mental health.

Dr. Rosenfeld is a member of the National Eating Disorders Association, the International Association of Eating Disorders Professionals, and the Academy for Eating Disorders, where she sits on the Social Media Committee.

She is active in the Los Angeles County Psychological Association, where she founded and chairs the Eating Disorder Special Interest Group.

She currently lives and practices in Southern California. She is also licensed to practice in New York and wishes she could be permanently bicoastal. You can reach her at www.staceyrosenfeld.com or www.eat-in-peace.com.